'THANK GOD I AM TRYING
TO DO MY LITTLE BIT'

'THANK GOD I AM TRYING TO DO MY LITTLE BIT'

Private Jim Elwell,
7th Battalion, the Suffolk Regiment.

A Walsall Lad's Letters from the Trenches
1916-1917

Editing and Commentary
by
Ken Wayman

TOMMIES GUIDES

Dedication

To all the descendants of Jim Elwell and in
memory of all the lads from near and far
who stood with him in the trenches and
tunnels at Arras.

Tommies Guides
Menin House
13 Hunloke Avenue
Eastbourne
East Sussex
BN22 8UL

www.tommiesguides.co.uk

Published by Tommies Guides, 2008

ISBN 0 95488 751 4

Cover design by Tommies Guides
Typeset by Graham Hales, Derby
Printed by Lightning Source Milton Keynes UK

Contents

List of Maps

List of Illustrations

Thanks and Acknowledgements

I would like to extend my grateful thanks to Elaine Cox for unlimited access to the papers of her great-grandfather, Jim Elwell, and access to numerous family photographs and memorabilia without which this book would never have seen the light of day.

I would also like to thank Elaine's mum, Marie, her Auntie Iris and her nan, Lucy (Jim Elwell's daughter) for their personal recollections of many of their relatives, friends and acquaintances. I must have been quite a pest at times!

I owe a debt of thanks to the dedicated volunteers at Pelsall History Centre in Church Road, Pelsall for much-needed help in tracing Jim Elwell's ancestors. They made a difficult task seem easy!

My thanks are also due to Phil Hazledine, the grandson of Jim Elwell's brother-in-law, Tom Spencer (married to Rose Elwell) with whom I came into contact via the 'Great War Forum' on Chris Baker's 'Long, Long Trail' website (a 'must' for anyone interested in any aspect of the Great War). Phil kindly offered me details of the Elwell/Spencer family that filled some not inconsiderable gaps in my research.

Graeme Clarke of Walsall Wood (and very local to me) also contacted me through Chris Baker's 'Great War Forum' offering me information about the likely date of Jim Elwell's transfer to 7th Suffolk. Evidently, a number of Walsall men from 1/6th South Staffordshire were posted to 7th Suffolk at the end of September and Graeme had a sound date for one of those men, Albert Stych, M.M. Graeme's welcome information is part of a yet unpublished book, a huge work that researches all of the Walsall men who were killed in the Great War – it deserves to be published as an important part of Walsall's history.

Yet another helping hand came from Steve Beard of Blackheath in the West Midlands. Again the contact came through the 'Great War Forum' but this time Steve managed to solve a puzzling problem that arose from one of Jim Elwell's letters – what was 'Sheen's'? Steve traced it to a baker of loaves and fancy cakes who ran a business in Park Street, Walsall. Many thanks, Steve.

Once more via the 'Great War Forum' came much-appreciated help from a stranger. Sharon Witherden very quickly found the solution to my query about a parcel service called 'Lazenby's' and thus solved a problem that cropped up in several of Jim's letters. Much appreciated, Sharon.

Again via the 'Forum', three lads offered to take photos of the headstones of Sid Powell (Ypres), Frank Townrow (Habarcq) and Harry Wassall (Laventie); my grateful thanks are due to Steve Morse, Jim McSharry and 'John K' whose full name has sadly (but predictably!) evaded my very fallible recording system. Sorry John!

Of course, I must offer my thanks to Chris Baker – without his superb website and its 'Great War Forum', many of my questions about Jim Elwell's letters would have remained unanswered. The Forum, which is free to use, is to be found at: www.1914-1918.net

If you are a Great War 'addict' like me you will enjoy this site!

Not long before the planned publication of this book I received two unexpected bonuses. The first came from Alleyn Jones, the great-granddaughter of Jim and MaryAnn Powell, who contacted me through the 'Great War Forum' with the kind offer of several photos of family members and a sketch of the Blue Lane houses drawn by her father, Fred Powell. Alleyn also kindly led me through the 'maze' of who's who in the related Powell and Elwell families. Both kindnesses are greatly appreciated. The second came through an excellent feature written by Robert Hardman of the 'Daily Mail'. A good friend of mine, Barry Crutchley, sent me the article (supplied by his Mum), entitled, 'City Under the Slaughter', which is a remarkable piece that details the development and employment of the caverns and extended tunnels under the city of Arras during the British offensive of April 1917. Mr. Hardman talked to me about the genesis of his work and most kindly allowed me to quote from his article. It is much appreciated.

One frustration is that I was unable to find those who hold the rights to 'F. Mackain's' superb cartoons in the 'Tommy' series of postcards. Without these illustrations the book would have been the poorer. Mackain's keen eye and sardonic humour captured the very essence of the Tommy's life.

Finally, I could never have produced this book without the wonderful letters written, often under difficult circumstances, by Jim Elwell – a man whose relatively ordinary life was rendered extraordinary by short-sighted politicians whose blunders had to be addressed by generals rather than diplomats. I hope this book does justice to his memory.

Foreword

The Kaiser thought his great army would sweep in to the sea that small force of British soldiers sent to help the French when war with Germany broke out on 4 August 1914. So sneering was he of the British Expeditionary Force that he commanded his forces to:

'exterminate first the treacherous English and walk over General French's contemptible little army'.

Massively outnumbered, yet the gallant British regulars were not overwhelmed. They proved to be tough and dogged opponents, who were skilled and swift marksmen with their Lee Enfields. My Grandad, Private Richard Alfred Chinn, number 9968, 2nd Battalion Coldstream Guards was one of those men who proudly called themselves the Old Contemptibles after the war.

He arrived in France on 13 August as part of the 4th (Guards) Brigade in the 2nd Division of I Corps. Five days later he wrote to his Mom in Alfred Street, Sparkbrook:

'We start this morning Tuesday for the front, sent out with rations and 120 rounds of ammunition each. Don't know wear we are for just yet let know later if we can. I don't think it will last long we are a happy Battalion of men and that's what the Germans are not. England for ever.'

On 23 August the 2nd Battalion crossed the Belgian border. By now Grandad and his pals were part of the 1st (Guards) Brigade in the newly-formed Guards Division, along with the 3rd Coldstreams, 2nd Grenadiers and 1st Irish. That day at the Battle of Mons the British showed their mettle, but faced with massive German superiority in numbers they had to retreat. Most of the heavy fighting involved troops of II Corps, which included the 1st Battalion Coldstream Guards; but soon the 2nd Battalion was involved in some big and important battles.

After the French with British support pushed back the Germans at the Battle of the Marne in early-September, the BEF locked horns with the enemy at the Battle of the Aisne. This began the trench warfare that so characterised the British experience of the First World War.

During that battle Grandad let his Mom know that he was still alive and well, although:

'we are having a rough time at present it has done nothing but rain for 5 days we have had plenty to do out here I will shake hands with myself if I get back in England after this, chaps who where in the South Africa said it was nothing to this we are at it every day here. General French congratulated us on the Guards work what we have done'.

A few days later Grandad urged his Mother not:

'to worry about me if it is my luck to go I go if not I live to tell the tale about it, we take no more notice of it than working in a factory it is our work we have got used to it.'

By early October the British forces were in Flanders, where for a month until 18 November, I Corps fought the bloody and bitter 1st Battle of Ypres. Five days before its end, Grandad told of a how his:

'arms ached through shooting so much and quick'

in repulsing one German attack. After the battle he proudly recounted how other soldiers declared that:

'there's no fear of Germans breaking through the lines when we are there, I saw in the paper a regiment were 9 days in the trenches we where 25 days and in half a foot of water at that.'

Soon after the 1st Battle of Ypres, Our Grandad was put in the Machine Gun Section of the 2nd Battalion of the Coldstream Guards. After a time 'resting' in routine marches and refitting, on 22 December, the Battalion set out for the trenches, which were in a terrible state owing to the continual rain. Many men were killed on Christmas Day itself. Our Grandad wrote to his Mom on 4 January that:

'we look like if we had a cartload of mud tipped on us, but the boys keep on smiling'.

His officer bought the lads a concertina and:

'when we go in the barns we have a little concert'.

A few days later Grandad recounted how:

'you have heard of the Germans and English being friends on Christmas Day, it was different in the trenches were the 4th Guards Brigade was for if you put your head above the trench you where a goner also if a German done the same his number would be up'.

As Grandad declared:

'we were the Guards Brigade where we was out to fight not to play with them as they have found'.

That letter was finished:

'good old Blues hard luck with the Villa''

At the end of January the Battalion moved to the brickfields at La Bassée. Sometime in February, Grandad was wounded badly in the knee joint and transferred to the Western and General Hospital, in Cardiff. On 18 March he told his Mom that:

'I shall be glad to see some of the old faces around the brook (Sparkbrook), but there will be a few missing who laid down their lives for England'.

Grandad's wound was too bad to allow him to go to back to the Front and eventually he came back to the Brook. When he died I was too young to have asked him questions. Luckily he left his letters so we know something of his war-time experiences and I know this: I am proud to be the grandson of an Old Contemptible.

Like my Grandad, Jim Elwell wrote back to his family, particularly to his beloved wife, Bertha. Unlike my Grandad, he wrote many letters, which now form a remarkable collection that has been kept carefully and lovingly by his family. And unlike my Grandad, sadly Jim did not come home. His wife, parents and loved ones had to endure months of anxiety over what had happened to him in the Battle of Arras in April 1917. First they were told that he was slightly wounded and then that he was missing and wounded. After months of fear, leavened occasionally by an almost bitter taste of hope, Jim's family had to accept that he was dead.

Still, Jim lives on and reaches out to us through his extraordinary correspondence – and above all it is his love for his family that calls out to us. Yes he mentions that there are plenty of rats in the trenches, that he is alive with livestock, that he has trench foot, that on occasions the action is 'warm', and that he is involved in fighting in which men die. Yet all this is written in a matter-of-fact way, as if these dreadful things were part and parcel of a job that had to be done – which to the British Tommy they were. What is more emotive is the way in which Jim tells of how he is glad that little Lucy is better, of how he urges Bertha not to worry so much and to be brave and bear it, and of how he assures his children that Daddy says they must be good little girls. These are the letters of a caring, compassionate man who through his love of his country is faced with the hardship of leaving behind all that he holds most close to his heart but who does so because he must do his duty.

Uncomplaining, dogged, thoughtful, loyal, steadfast, certain of God's love and that of his family and above all, giving: that was Jim Elwell. His dear wife yearned for the day when he could come home and they could share their love and their lives again. That day never came – but Jim is with his family still, through what he wrote. His great granddaughter, Elaine Cox, is the custodian of his letters and those of his wife, Bertha. Elaine has allowed them to be brought to a wider audience through the skills of Ken Wayman. Ken has allowed Jim to speak for himself but has embedded his letters within the broader contexts of time and place, so enabling us to understand all the better Jim and his family and their place in the First World War. A sensitive and talented researcher, Ken lets us see Jim Elwell as he is and in so doing he brings a face to the host of men who served their country. Through Jim we can see all those other Tommies who died in the Western Front. Jim Elwell was a true Englishman. May he and all those others who died in the First World War rest in God's peace.

Professor Carl Chinn MBE
(Birmingham, May 2008)

Author's Introduction

This is the story of Isaac James 'Jim' Elwell, a story that is both ordinary and remarkable. It is an ordinary story in that it is similar to that of thousands of other Walsall lads who went off to fight in the Great War of 1914-1918; it is ordinary in that Jim was a soldier for only eleven months, took part in just two major set-piece attacks, spent most of his time in France involved in the trench soldier's endless round of front line/support/reserve/rest and, like so many others, was allowed no home leave; he received the British War Medal and the Victory Medal like millions of others who left these shores; just like most of them he constantly worried about his family and friends, detested the trenches but always felt he had to 'do his bit' and 'keep smiling.'

Yet his story is remarkable in that it is one of the not-so-many private soldiers' stories that are recorded for posterity. From the document of attestation in December 1915 indicating his willingness to join up when his turn came, from a stream of letters and field service postcards from the Western Front, from a few of his wife, Bertha's, returned letters and ultimately from the heart-rending casualty and bureaucratic pension letters, we are able to trace Jim's service to King and Country and how it affected his close-knit family. His letters lead us from the Walsall Recruiting Office in Park Street to Scotton Training Camp near Catterick in Yorkshire and thence to the Western Front in France. Once 'out there', we learn of the rigours of trench life, of transfers and attachment to other units and of Jim's views on his bit of the war and on the war in general. Although rarely graphic in their language, Jim's letters provide clear evidence of the tragic side of life in the front line as he writes of family, friends and acquaintances who 'went under' or 'went west' – a soldier rarely actually referred to 'being killed.'

Yet Jim was far more than a soldier – he was a son, a husband, a father, a brother, a workmate and a good friend. His letters reveal a man much more concerned with those left behind than with the decisions of the red-tabbed staff officers who would ultimately send him to his death on a cold Arras hillside. Jim was far more sanguine about facing 'Fritz' than he was about being away from his beloved wife, Bertha, and from his two lovely, little daughters, Lizzie and Lucy. He constantly asked for news of his relatives, friends and work colleagues, hoping against hope that 'their turn' would not come round too soon – Jim knew what the front line was like and did not want those who were close to him to experience it. Unfortunately, many of them would do just that.

Following Jim's death in April 1917, a 'wounded and missing in action' situation complicated by confusing messages from those in army authority, Bertha's struggle to ascertain her husband's fate may be witnessed and finally, though still expecting him to come home, so may that of going through the finality of the bureaucratic nightmare of obtaining an army pension.

All too often, stories of the Great War concentrate upon the horrific scale of the conflict rather than upon the individuals who fought in it. This is an individual's story. This is Private Jim Elwell's story.

Ken Wayman (*Pelsall, May 2008*)

Arras Town Hall, showing the effects of heavy German shelling. This landmark would have been familiar to Private Jim Elwell whose unit, 7th Battalion, the Suffolk Regiment, was frequently in the reserve lines in the town of Arras.

Jim Elwell, Walsall, summer 1916.

MAP ONE

Arras sector, October 1916 to April 1917 – front line, support, reserve, rest and training locations of 7th Battalion, the Suffolk Regiment

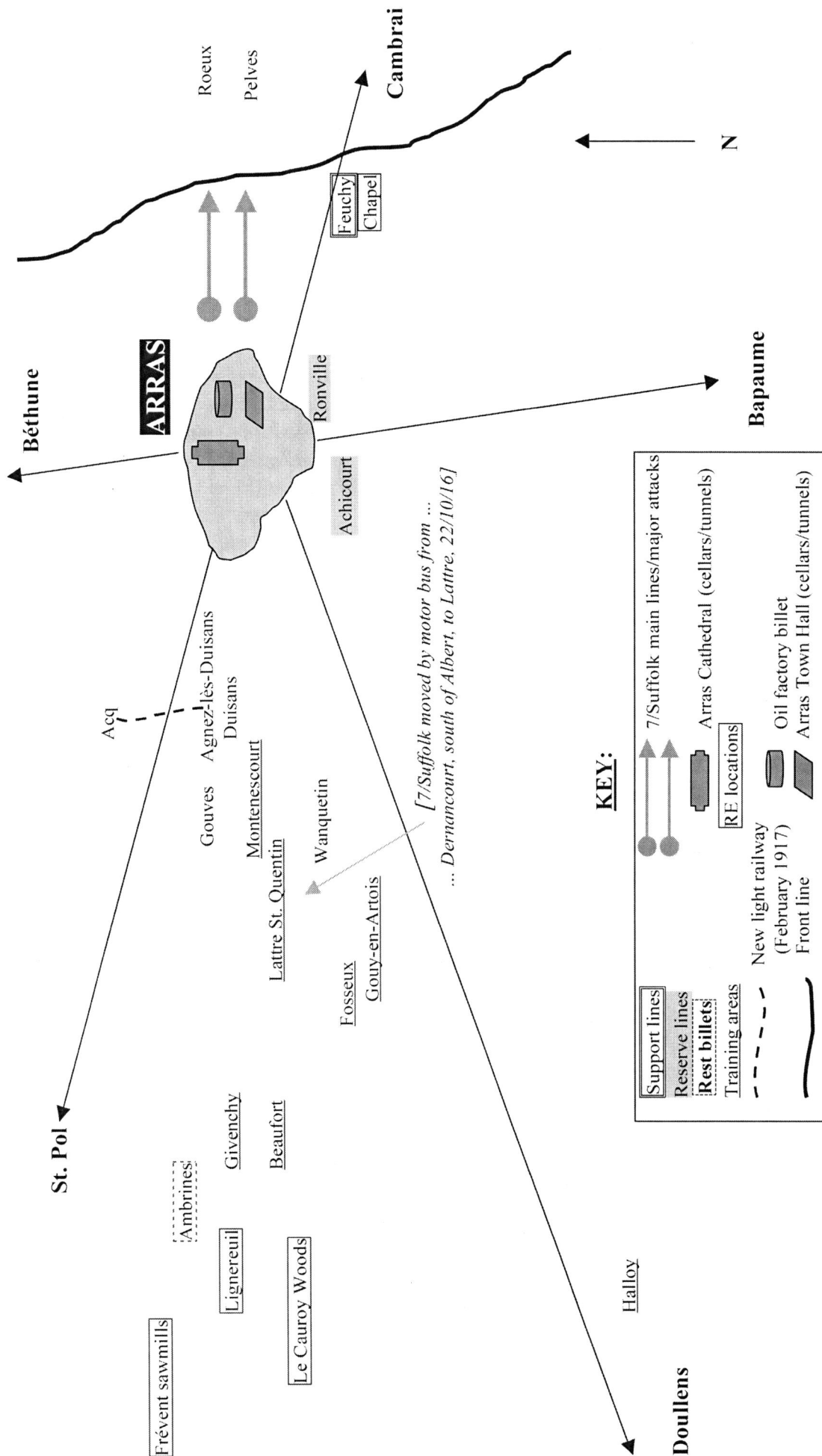

Roeux
Pelves

Cambrai

N

Feuchy Chapel

Béthune

ARRAS

Ronville

Achicourt

Bapaume

Acq

Agnez-lès-Duisans

Gouves   Duisans

Montenescourt

Wanquetin

Lattre St. Quentin

Fosseux
Gouy-en-Artois

[7/Suffolk moved by motor bus from … … Dernancourt, south of Albert, to Lattre, 22/10/16]

St. Pol

Ambrines

Givenchy

Lignereuil

Beaufort

Le Cauroy Woods

Frévent sawmills

Halloy

Doullens

KEY:

7/Suffolk main lines/major attacks

Arras Cathedral (cellars/tunnels)

RE locations

Oil factory billet
Arras Town Hall (cellars/tunnels)

Support lines
Reserve lines
Rest billets:
Training areas

New light railway (February 1917)
Front line

CHAPTER ONE
'Before this cruel war'

Although Jim Elwell had lived in Walsall since before his second birthday, his family were in fact Birmingham people. His paternal grandfather, Isaac Elwell, was born in Coleshill in Warwickshire in about 1820 but had been living in the Whitechapel area of London for several years when his two eldest sons, Henry and Joseph Benjamin (Jim's father), were born. Isaac's wife, Elizabeth, was a Birmingham girl and Isaac was by trade a gun-maker, so it was logical that they made the move back to their home city, a move that occurred in the mid-1850's. Once settled back in the heart of the Midlands, the couple had at least three more children, William, Isaac and MaryAnn. By 1871, Joseph had married Martha Wassall, a Black Country girl, had left home, started his own family and was resident at number 6, Back of Rawlins Street in the Ladywood area of Birmingham. At that time, Joseph appears to have been working in an iron foundry as a puddler, a hot, physical job; his eldest daughter, also named Martha, was born in West Bromwich but his eldest son, Joseph Henry, was born in Birmingham in 1871. As the years passed, so more youngsters arrived; Elizabeth was born in about 1873, MaryAnn in about 1875, Rosetta (known as Rose) in about 1877 before Isaac James (known to the world as Jim) made his first appearance on 3rd October 1879 when the family was living at 1, Upper Court Street in Birmingham. Within two years, the family had left Birmingham and moved the few miles north to number 9, Forge Street in Walsall and Jim's father had changed his employment, becoming an engine driver – the two facts are more than probably linked. However, soon after moving, the family had suffered a terrible but not uncommon tragedy. On 8th August 1880 Jim's older brother, nine year-old Joseph Henry, had drowned in the Birmingham Canal near Dalkeith Street; sadly, he was not to be the only one of the Elwell lads to die before his time.

In Walsall, more young Elwells arrived to fill the house – Lucy was born in about 1882, Florence Ellen (known as Nellie) in about 1886 and Joseph Edward (later to be known as Ted) in about 1888. On 21st July 1889, at the age of almost ten, Jim Elwell was baptised at the local Primitive Methodist Church, though interestingly his name was written as 'James Isaac' rather than the 'Isaac James' of his birth certificate. Jim's father had again changed employment and was working as a labourer and the family had moved house once again, to Green Lane, in the Birchills area of Walsall. However, by the autumn of 1889 the family had moved house yet again, probably to accommodate the growing brood, this time taking up residence at 93, Farringdon Street, Walsall. The evidence for this latter move is a Labour Certificate awarded to Jim Elwell on his tenth birthday stating that he,

> '...has received (a certificate) from one of Her Majesty's Inspectors of Schools, that he (James Elwell) has reached the V Standard... reached means passed in reading, writing and arithmetic,'

but frustratingly the document gives no indication of the school that Jim attended. The house in which the family lived must have been of a fair size as by 1891 it accommodated not only the youngsters but also eldest daughter, Martha, and her new husband, Joe Boddice, a coal miner who hailed from Wolverhampton. In addition to Joe and Martha, mother Martha's thirty-two year old brother, James Wassall, was also resident as a lodger (Martha had at least one other brother, Henry); it may have made the place a little crowded but it would certainly have helped with the finances.

The turn of the century saw changes in the Elwell household. By 1901, yet another move had taken the family to 54, Dalkeith Street, again in the Birchills area of Walsall, though the house was apparently somewhat smaller as it was by then accommodating just parents Joseph and Martha along with Jim, Lucy, Nell and Ted, of whom only young Ted was still at school. Joseph was now a self-employed milk-

Bertha Webster.

vendor, selling his wares from a wheeled barrow that he pushed round Walsall – Jim Elwell's daughter, Lucy, remembers in later years helping her grandad on his milk round. Joseph's wife, Martha, kept a small general store in Dalkeith Street that sold, in Lucy's words, *'…just about everything.'* As for twenty-one year old Jim, he was working as a packer, possibly already employed by Albert and S.B. Jagger of Green Lane, Walsall, a job that would last until his enlistment in the army; Jim's younger sisters were both employed in the famed Walsall leather industry, Lucy as a bridle-stitcher and Nell as a whip-varnisher.

1908 proved to be a momentous year for Jim Elwell. On 26th September, at St. Patrick's Roman Catholic Church in Walsall, he was married to Bertha Webster, one of ten children to William and Sarah Webster. Father John Roskell conducted the ceremony while the principal witnesses were Sid Powell and Nell Elwell, all three of whom in later years would figure large in Jim's letters from the trenches. Jim and Bertha set up home at 42, Blue Lane West in Walsall (shown below). Their house, owned by Fred Powell (Sid's brother) who lived next door with his wife, Teresa, was then considered good quality as it had an upstairs bathroom with gas geysers to supply hot water and a well in the brew-house (scullery) to provide fresh, cold water. The following year, on 22nd September 1909, the marriage was blessed by the arrival of Elizabeth Hilda,

41 and 42 Blue Lane West, either side of the main arch. Jim Elwell lived at 42 and Fred Powell lived at 41. At the rear of number 41 was the foundry owned and worked by Fred Powell. The sketch was drawn by Jim Powell's son, Fred.

who would be known to everyone as Lizzie. Eighteen months later, Lizzie was joined by a little sister, Lucy Marie, who came into the world on 25th March 1911. Together, the two girls were to be Jim's pride and joy – the *'little' uns'* of his letters from the trenches.

Jim Elwell.

As the years passed, Jim (right) became a valued worker at the lorinery (sad-dlery ironmongery) business in Green Lane of Mr. Albert Jagger and his son, Mr. S.B. Jagger. Exactly what was Jim's job in the firm is a matter for specu-lation but in letters he frequently spoke of, *'…the shop':*

'I have had three (letters) from the shop this week, one each from the two young girls, one from the lad and one (also) from Mr. Case.' *[1st July 1916]*

'If you go to the shop remember me to them all.' *[12th November 1916]*

'And how are all my mates at the shop?' *[16th November 1916]*

When Jim went off to join the army, Mr. Albert Jagger and his son proved themselves most benevolent employers, not only to Jim but also to Bertha as she struggled to make ends meet in Jim's absence. Mr. Jagger took the trouble to keep in touch with Jim and was generous in what he sent to France:

'Dear Bertha, I have just had a New Year card from S B Jagger – it's a very nice one too and he tells me he sent me a parcel a week before this card was posted.' *[28th December 1916]*

'I have received a parcel from Mr. Jagger and very good one too. It had some Christmas pudding in, some fags, a tin of peaches and a lot of other things. I have written to him to thank him for it.' *[1st January 1916]*

Moreover, he went out of his way to give as much help as he could muster to ease Bertha's later dealings with bureaucracy:

'You need not worry about Mr. Jagger – I will write him to thank him for his kindness.' *[10th February 1917]*

'Dear Bertha, let me know how you get on with that little affair, you know what I mean, the one Mr. Jagger is looking into for you and please let me know how you get on.' *[15th February 1917]*

'Dear Bertha, you were vexed, I know, when you knew you had failed by not getting what you wanted but don't grieve over it, old girl, you tried your best and lost. It was very kind of Mr. Jagger to make the running for you – I will write to him to thank him for his trouble. I dare say he wishes I were back with him. So do I, as we always got on well together – the others often wondered how it was (so).'   [8th March 1917]

However, Albert Jagger himself had evidently received a nasty surprise during November 1916 when his son was called up:

'How's Mr. Wood getting on without SBJ? Where has he gone to and how's he getting on with army life? He will find it a bit different to sitting in his office and running about up and down stairs.'   [12th November 1916]

Little is known of S.B. Jagger's army career (although he certainly survived) but it did not stop his father sending a Christmas parcel to Jim in December!

As his letters from the trenches will clearly show, Jim was a devout member of the Catholic Church, regularly attending St. Patrick's in Walsall. However, as has been indicated, Jim was baptised in the Primitive Methodist Church, thus it is most likely that he happily converted to Catholicism as a result of his relationship with Bertha, who came from a staunch Catholic family. Yet once he was in the trenches it was rare for Jim to enjoy the ministrations of a Catholic priest, as his letter of Sunday, 4th November clearly demonstrates:

'I wish I was having my Sunday breakfast at home. About this time, I should be getting ready for Church. I haven't been for weeks – I wish I could. They had Church for the Church of England chaps before we went in the trenches but I didn't go – I wanted to go to my own, else none at all.'   [4th November 1916]

Sometime prior to Jim's induction into the ways of the military, his parish priest, Fr. John Roskell, presented the lad with a rosary; it is not difficult to imagine Jim's emotions on the day he realised that he had lost the attached crucifix:

'I forgot to tell you I lost the crucifix off those (rosary) beads Fr. Roskell gave me – I can't find it anywhere. I am vexed about it because you know I honour and respect the one who gave them to me. Bertha, remember me to Fr. McDonell and Fr. Clavin and to all those men at the Church.'   [12th November 1916]

Jim's respect for Fr. Roskell is crystal clear but his opinion of Fr. McDonell is shown in a rather back-handed compliment:

'…you will think I am always begging off you but I am like Fr.Mac(Donell) – he don't know how to beg but he has got a very good way of asking his people which always seems to get a splendid response.'
                                [7th April 1917]

Jim was very aware that many of the men from St. Patrick's were, like himself, fighting for King and Country, and that among them a heavy price was being paid [more than one hundred were to die, their names commemorated on the St. Patrick's Roman Catholic Church Roll of Honour shown on page 85]:

'How are all the folks at home and my friends at the Church? Please remember me to them all.'
                            [30th January 1917]

'…remember me to all I know, also to the men at the Church – there are very few left now, I guess.'
                            [31st March 1917]

Those still left in the congregation at St. Patrick's had, most certainly, not forgotten Jim and demonstrated their concern in a most appropriate and appreciated manner:

'I am also glad to say I have received the parcel from Church – a khaki shirt and a pair of socks. I shan't wear them here; if I can I shall send them home. Will you thank them for me please? Tell them I shall need their prayers but if they pray for me I shall pray for them. God bless them all.'   [21st December 1916]

As will be seen, prayer and an enduring faith were to be among the few constants that would sustain Jim in the front line, the horrors of which the world had never previously witnessed.

Family photograph taken at Nell Elwell's wedding to Will Simpson (c.1910):

Key to the family photograph

Photograph taken on the occasion of Nell Elwell's marriage to Will Simpson [c. 1909-1912] –

Jim Elwell	(seated 3rd from left)
Ted Elwell	(seated far left)
Will and Nell Simpson	(seated 4th and 5th from left)
Lucy Elwell	(seated 4th from right)
Patti and Martha Boddice	(seated 3rd and 2nd from right)
Tom Spencer	(standing, back, 5th from left)
Nellie Webster	(behind bride, immediately right)
Phoebe Boddice	(next to Nellie Webster, to right of bride)
Henry Wassall	(back, 3rd from right)
Joe Boddice	(back, far right).'

Note: Jim's wife, Bertha, is missing from the picture – this might be at the time of Lucy's birth. At Jim's knee is possibly a very young Lizzie.

CHAPTER TWO

'...it's got to be done when you're in the Army'

The British Expeditionary Force (B.E.F.) that was sent to France in August and September of 1914 comprised just six divisions of infantry, fewer than 100,000 effective rifles that constituted a mere drop in the ocean compared to the forces of their French allies. Facing them was a German Army bolstered by a tradition of universal conscription and, by mid-August 1914, numbering nearly four million men in the field (though necessarily divided between the Western Front in France and Flanders, and the Eastern Front in Russia). In the light of Britain's urgent need for recruits Lord Kitchener, the newly-appointed Secretary of State for War and himself probably the country's most famous soldier, decided to raise an entire new army. Kitchener appealed for men to step forward, hoping for 100,000 to volunteer in the following six months. The response is near-legend – 500,000 men offered their services in the very *first* month of recruiting! Initially the army's ability to cope with the sheer volume of men was quite overwhelmed but as the months passed deep into 1915, so the new battalions were to grow into new divisions, and new divisions ultimately were to become a new army. Kitchener's 'New Army', though raised from civilians taken from every class and walk of life and officered largely by 'dugouts'[1] and fresh-faced public schoolboys, was to prove to be the anvil upon which eventual victory was fashioned. The old year of 1914 turned into the new one of 1915 and the surge of recruits topped the one million mark but the struggle to stem the grey tide of the German advance on Paris had taken its toll of the original British Expeditionary Force. Constantly on the back foot after the first major clash on the canal at Mons in Belgium, the ensuing general retreat, although controlled and effective, was not without great cost – a cost that had became unsustainable following the successive battles of the Marne, the Aisne, Armentières and First Ypres. In short the small, professional army of the B.E.F. had virtually bled to death by Christmas 1914. Only slowly was the gap plugged by the recruits of August 1914 and by the much-derided 'weekend soldiers' of the Territorial Force[2], most of whom had willingly foregone their right to serve only within the United Kingdom.

However, by the late autumn of 1915, battles such as Neuve Chapelle (March), 2nd Ypres (April/May), Aubers Ridge (May), Festubert (May) and Loos (September/October) had inflicted on the British Army losses to the tune of almost 400,000 men, while the earlier flood of voluntary recruitment for Regular, Territorial and New Army battalions had slowed to a relative trickle. In December 1915, volunteers numbered just 55,000, whereas during the Battle of Loos in September-October 1915, the British had sustained upwards of 50,000 casualties; furthermore, Scottish and Irish regiments, with their smaller home populations to draw upon, were finding it increasingly difficult to fill the widening gaps in the ranks. Across the board, in the wake of major engagements, battalions that had had an original establishment of a thousand men whilst in barracks in Britain now witnessed roll-calls to which only three or four hundred men answered. Pressure on the authorities was mounting.

The government's considered response in October 1915 was to appoint Lord Derby to the post of Director General of Recruiting. Derby, a prominent opponent of conscription, had come to popular attention in August 1914 when he made a vigorous appeal in Liverpool for work colleagues, friends and sports club members to volunteer together on the proviso that they would serve together. Thus was born the concept of what would become known to posterity as the 'Pals Battalions'. Yet even the numbers generated by the 'Pals' idea could not satisfy the needs of an army that was suffering unconscionable casualties in battle, in routine trench-holding and from chronic illness and injury. So Lord Derby initiated a scheme whereby men of military age

---

[1] 'Dugout' was a familiar term used to describe retired officers who were 'dug out' from retirement to lend their experience to the new 'war service' battalions.
[2] Lord Kitchener had initially rejected the service of the Territorials with the terse phrase, 'I don't want Territorials, I want soldiers!' Fortunately for the country, the Territorial battalions were to fight and distinguish themselves side by side with both Regular and New Army battalions.

could attest their willingness to serve when their 'turn' came; for their part, the government promised to call upon single men first in an attempt to allow married men to settle their family affairs before being called up. The result of the Derby Scheme was to induce more than 2,800,000[3] men to attest between 23rd October and 15th December 1915. Jim Elwell was one of these men who answered Lord Derby's call.

No evidence has survived pertaining to Jim's reasoning behind his decision to attest in December 1915 but it probably owed much to the government's promise to take married men last of all. Jim had two young daughters and joining the army would surely knock a sizeable hole in the family budget, so he would likely have decided against volunteering earlier in the war as he was fearful of the effect it might have upon his beloved family. Whatever the realities, Jim finally decided to attest his willingness to serve on Wednesday, 8th December 1915. His attestation card (below) was stamped, '38th Recruiting Area, Recruiting Office, Walsall. 75, Park Street, Walsall', an office that had been in existence at least since the outbreak of war in August 1914. On the card, Jim is named as, 'Isaac Elwell of 42, Blue Lane West, Walsall,' and as holder of, 'Armlet 050518. No. 85, group no. 42.'[4] His commitment, and the circumstances under which he would be called up, were clearly set out as follows on the Attestation Card:-

'The above-named man has been attested and transferred to the Army Reserve, until required for service, when he will be sent a Notice Paper, informing him as to the date, time and place at which he is to report himself. Fourteen days' notice will be given.'

Signed by the major.

Jim Elwell's attestation card.

That 'fourteen days' notice' was given in mid-1916 and Jim Elwell was thus called up for his army service, according to the 'Walsall Observer', in June 1916. Initially, he reported to the South Staffordshire Regimental Depot at Whittington Barracks near Lichfield and from there was sent with his draft to Scotton Camp at Catterick in Yorkshire. It was at Scotton that civilian Jim Elwell began the recently foreshortened process of army training that was to turn him into Private I.J. Elwell, 5937, 16 Platoon, 'D' Company, 6th South Staffordshire Reserve Battalion and set him on a road that would lead to the Somme and Arras on the Western Front – a road that would ultimately lead to a destination with death.

As soon as Jim was notified of his call-up, the bureaucratic wheels jerked into motion to verify that he was actually married and actually had two children – a process implemented for the purpose of assessing the amount of Separation Allowance that was due to the family. Bertha sent off all the requisite certificates and must have been pleasantly surprised by their prompt return from the Secretary of the South Staffordshire Territorial Force Association Separation Department in Stafford. Dated June 30th 1916, the letter read:

'Dear Madam, I return forthwith – marriage certificate and birth certificates for two children, the necessary particulars having been extracted.

Yours etc, Capt., sec., Staffs TFA.'

Precisely when Jim left home for Yorkshire and kept his date with the training corporals of Catterick is not known but the first surviving letter to his wife Bertha, his 'little' uns', Lizzie and Lucy, and Granny, was written on a day that is forever burned deep into the mind of the British people – Saturday, 1st July 1916. While Jim was trying to adapt to the strictures of army life, the cream of the 'Pals' battalions of the New Army along with many famous Regular Army battalions were going 'over the top' of the parapets of trenches on the Somme into an unrelenting storm of machine gun and artillery fire. As the sun set on that hot yet chilling summer's day, the British army on the Somme had suffered nearly sixty thousand casualties and a deadly, five-month grinding battle had commenced. Jim would be in France[5] long before the interminable, draining battles of the Somme dragged to their muddy conclusion on

---

[3] From among an estimated 5,000,000 men of military age (18 years to 41 years).
[4] The armlet was intended to identify men who had attested and helped them to avoid being given the 'white feather of cowardice' that some women were then handing out in the hope of persuading men of military service age to volunteer.
[5] Jim's first posting, to 1/6th Battalion, the South Staffordshire Regiment, took him to Berles-au-Bois and Bailleulmont, on the northern extremity of the Somme sector – see Chapter Three.

the Ancre in mid-November. Jim, like the rest of the population, was utterly unaware of what was happening on that fateful day on the Somme and logically concerned himself with explaining to his dear family the beginnings of his new life in khaki.

[Notes on the letters, postcards and field service postcards:

Eighty-three original letters remain in the care of Jim Elwell's family; fifty-two were written by Jim and five by Bertha, while the balance were written to Bertha by relatives, friends and official organisations. For convenience, each of the letters is numbered though this should not be taken to mean that other letters were not sent apart from those that still exist – for example, the vast majority of letters from Bertha to Jim have not survived. Where a word or words appear in round brackets, it is simply to help clarify the original writer's sentence. Anything written in square brackets is additional information intended to put the writer's words in a broader context – I trust these additions will not spoil the reader's enjoyment. Every one of the letters sent by Jim from France was written using pencil and, although some of the words are occasionally smudged or faded, the vast majority of Jim's words have survived the years remarkably well.

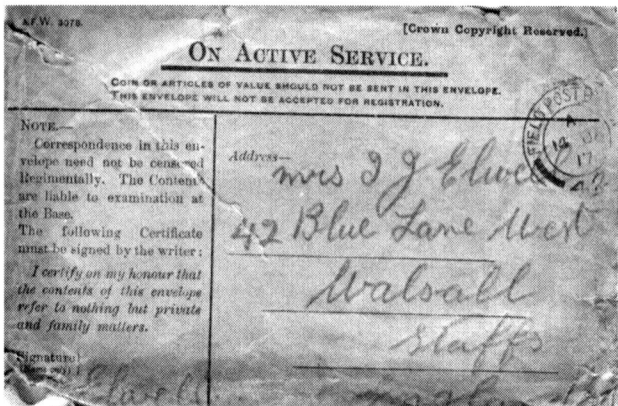

Cover of the 'private' Green Envelope.

However, the 'blue pencil' of the official army censor loomed large in every soldier's letter-writing life. Early in the war, some soldiers serving on the Western Front had sent letters direct to their local newspapers describing their unit's exploits in the trenches but, as direction of the war itself became tighter, so did control of what might be written from the front. Of crucial importance was avoiding any information that might prove of use to the enemy, so soldiers' letters came under the direct scrutiny of a 'censor'. For the most part, letters were opened and checked for 'sensitive' information by a man's immediate officer – anything 'suspect' was crossed through. Many officers disliked this role as they frequently came across very personal passages in their men's communications. As the war progressed, the army instituted two remarkably good ideas – the

'green envelope' and the 'field service postcard', both of which are shown here (left and below). A soldier was entitled to a 'green envelope' every month or so and he was put on trust not to include in the enclosed letter anything that might be of use to an enemy, such as a unit's location, actions or strength; in return, the letter, '…need not be censored regimentally', though, '…the contents are liable to examination at the base.' The writer had to sign a certificate on the front of the envelope confirming, 'I certify on my honour that

Cover of the Field Service Postcard.

the contents of this envelope refer to nothing but private and family matters.' It thus enabled a man to write his more personal thoughts without having his immediate officer read them, although a sample number of these envelopes were opened at the base, '…to check the level of morale among the troops'. The 'field service postcard' was a simple but effective scheme. A man, usually in the trenches, could just delete inappropriate phrases from a printed list, sign the card and send it down the line. Although any added information would lead to the card being destroyed, it did keep families in some sort of contact and was thus beneficial to a man's morale.]

LETTER 1

[Saturday 1 July 1916. Written to Bertha and the girls and Granny. It is headed, 'Pte IJ Elwell, 5937, 16 Platoon, 'D' Coy[6], 6th South Staffordshire Reserve, Scotton Camp, Catterick, Yorkshire.']

In all of his letters, Jim's first and abiding concern was for his family and friends:

'Just a line in answer to your kind letter. Thanks very much for the postal order. I am pleased to hear that my little Lucy is better and Ted [Jim's brother who was already in khaki and had either been ill or wounded] too. I hope the letter will find you, Lizzie and Granny well in health as it leaves me.'

---

[6] 'Coy' is an abbreviation for 'company', a sub-unit of a battalion. There were normally four 'line' or 'rifle' companies [A, B, C, D] and a smaller Head Quarters company per battalion; line companies at full strength comprised about 240 men. Within each company in the field were four platoons, each containing 50-60 men.

Wherever Jim found himself, whether in England or France, he always tried to seek out little keepsakes and cards to send home to Bertha and the girls; Catterick was no exception:

'I hope you have received the brooches I sent you and the kiddies.'

A recurring theme in Jim's letters is how his wife was managing in her much straitened circumstances, occasionally gently chiding Bertha for her generosity in her parcels to him. Jim was well aware that his absence had put a strain upon the family budget and he constantly spoke of this:

'Dear Bertha, you didn't say whether you had had your money alright this week...you should have £1..1s. a week.'

Considering that the 'Rowntree Report'[7] of 1899 estimated that 'poverty line' income was £1 .. 1s. a week, the income of the Elwell household was worryingly low and Jim was acutely aware of it. His early letters reflect the novelty of army life and routine, not always for the best:

'Dear Bertha, don't build on me coming home yet – some say we have vaccination leave, some say we don't. (In fact) I have just heard that we have to be inoculated again on Tuesday but they say I shan't feel the next dose, at least they say so if you feel it very bad first time and I know I did.'

The dreaded army 'jabs' were not the only things that erstwhile civilian Jim was finding not entirely to his taste:

'Don't worry about the washing – they see that you are all clean here. They inspect you every morning when we go on C.O. (Commanding Officer's) Battalion Parade – they look at your buttons, your boots, your tunic, your putties (puttees), hat-badges and see that your face has been shaved. If any of these haven't been done they tell you about it and the next time they tell you it's clink for you. So you see it takes us all our spare time to keep our things clean – it's got to be done when you're in the Army.'

Though not really enjoying the process, Jim was already coming round to the view that there was no point in fighting the army's way of doing things – better to get it done sooner rather than later. Jim was also aware of the rapid turnover in personnel in the training battalion:

'They are sending men up here every week from somewhere and they are sending big drafts away to France every week. Dear Bertha, you will find I told you about young Joe [most likely a Walsall lad that Jim knew from pre-war days] going away in my last letter. I went down to see him off but I was too late – they had gone about five minutes before I got there. Hard lines, wasn't it? I treated him well, the short time I had with him. He was second 'waiting-man' – they go down with them and if one man falls out while they are going to the station, well, these 'waiting-men' have to take their place. Silly young fool, he could have come back because there was only one man fell out and young Joe was the second 'waiting-man'....but he asked them to let him go and they did. God bless him and I hope he'll do well. He's always talking about Ted [Jim's brother] being out there and I think he thinks of him a lot.'

Jim Powell, Jim Elwell's brother-in-law.

It never becomes apparent who 'young Joe' actually was, though the reference to, 'always talking about Ted,' might suggest that he was Joe Boddice, Jim's brother-in-law and his sister Martha's husband. Jim, as always thinking of others, also commented:

'I'm glad they haven't taken Jim Powell (above) – I didn't think they would.'

Jim Powell was married to Bertha's sister, Mary Ann, and was Fred and Sid Powell's brother; the latter was a witness at Jim and Bertha's wedding. There is a story behind Jim Elwell's comment, '...I didn't think they would (take him).' As a youngster, Jim Powell was the victim of an unfortunate incident when a large stone was recklessly thrown over a wall; it hit Jim in the chest, collapsing one of his lungs – a serious injury in the early

[7] Seebohm Rowntree (ancestor of the confectionery company family) commissioned an inquiry into, and wrote a report upon, poverty in the city of York in 1899. Among his conclusions was that twenty-one shillings then constituted what he called 'the poverty line.'

1900's and one that most likely explains Jim being excluded from the military. Neither does the story end there. In 1918 Jim contracted Spanish 'flu during the dreadful pandemic and, weakened by the chest injury of his youth, sadly died at the age of just thirty.

Jim Elwell never missed a chance to ask to be remembered to friends and family, though he always apologised in advance for not having the time or resources to write personally to each of them:

'Dear Bertha, remember me to Jack Jurdy [this name is not clear whenever it is mentioned in Jim's letters] and to Annie and to Florry Russell – I don't know her married name. Has Mrs. Partridge got the lad now? Remember me to your Mother [Sarah Webster], Sid and Maria [Powell], (their son) young Sid [Powell], to Jim [Powell, his brother-in-law] and my Nan [Elizabeth Elwell], to Sophia [Swain, Bertha's sister] and [husband] Fred [Swain], Harry [probably Webster, Jim's brother-in-law] and Alice [Powell, who married Henry Webster] and to Fred and Teresa [Powell, who owned 42, Blue Lane in which Jim and Bertha lived and themselves lived next door]. Remember me to all I know and tell them I shall be pleased receive letters from any of them but I can't write back to them all. I have had three (letters) from the shop this week, one each from the two young girls, one from the lad and one from Mr. Case [again, this name is far from clear]. So you see, I am not forgotten – the chaps in the hut say I am the top for letters – I am glad as it shows they haven't forgotten me.'

The 'shop' referred to in the letter is almost certainly that owned by Mr. Albert Jagger and his son, Mr. S.B. Jagger, in which Jim worked prior to his enlistment in 1916. Judging by the number of individuals mentioned in various letters, it would appear that Mr. Jagger's lorinery (saddlery ironmongery) business was quite substantial.

Jim invariably signed off with love to Bertha and to his 'little'uns', usually sending lots of kisses to share among the three of them. Most letters were also accompanied by a blessing or, more frequently in later months, a prayer:

'I send my very best love to you and the little'uns and Granny.
From your loving husband and Daddy xxxxxxx.
Plenty for you all.
God bless you all.'

Army Basic Training at Catterick

By the summer of 1916, army training facilities in the United Kingdom had fully recovered from the overwhelming flood of recruits in autumn 1914 and had developed an effective network across the country, from Salisbury Plain to Cannock Chase and Catterick.

13 Platoon 6th South Staffordshire Reserve at Scotton Camp. Jim is kneeling second left, front; Alf Walker is second right, front.

On arrival at Scotton Camp, Jim Elwell would have been issued with his army kit for which he became responsible; often ill-fitting, the boots, uniform and webbing had to be kept in pristine condition, requiring monotonously long hours of attention. Day on day, physical fitness was built up as were the near-automatic responses on the drill square; above all discipline was hammered home – individual discipline, group discipline, march discipline, weapons discipline and, above all, self-discipline.

Within his unit, every soldier would have to learn basic field-craft skills and musketry, then more specialised skills specific to his role; many men received initial training to equip them as signallers, bombers, machine gunners and the like. Finally, as the day approached for a man's draft to prepare for overseas service, the troops were given their first taste of front line survival skills in trench digging, wiring and revetting, anti-gas defence and very basic first aid.

By Jim Elwell's time, the training course had been pared to just three months in comparison to the six-month course that had greeted the first of Kitchener's recruits in August 1914. In just twelve weeks at basic training camp it was deemed that civilians taken from the full spectrum of jobs and backgrounds were ready to face the harsh rigours of trench warfare. As Jim would find out, they would all still have much to learn the hard way in the mud of France and Flanders.

SOUVENIR LETTER CARD 2

[Sunday 2 July 1916. Written to Bertha and the girls and Granny. This is a Souvenir Letter Card of Richmond, Yorkshire. It is headed, 'Pte IJ Elwell, 5937, 16 Platoon, 'D' Coy, 6th South Staffs Reserve, Scotton Camp, Catterick, Yorkshire.']

Bertha had obviously gotten into the habit of sending Jim copies of the local paper, although which one is never made clear:

> 'Thanks for the papers – I shall have something to read now,'

suggesting that Jim's indication of all spare time being taken by cleaning was something of a soldier's exaggeration! Local papers from home forged a link of normality for the average Tommy, whether in training or at the front. The idea of no free time is further undermined by the fact that the card was sent from Richmond on a day out! Jim had evidently already made some good friends and enjoyed spending his leisure time with them:

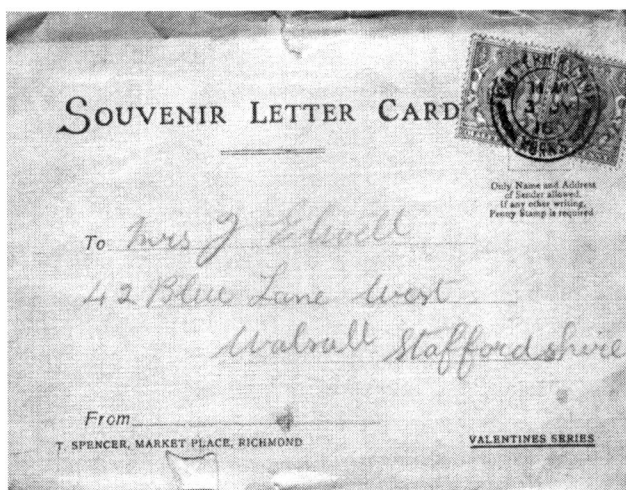

Souvenir letter card of Richmond, Yorkshire, containing ten views of the town.

> 'There are views of Richmond [ten connected postcards in a folding cover, shown above] – I have just come back from there. I went with about six other chaps out of our hut and a good and jolly lot of chaps they were, some of the best that any chap could wish to be with [see the 13 Platoon photograph on page 22]. I wish it had been Saturday (as) mostly all the shops were closed and I could not get anything.'

Jim signs off the second letter in his usual, affectionate manner but reminds his wife, Bertha, that:

> '....I don't wish for you to answer all these letters.... because I know you haven't the time,'

though he was not averse to asking for other friends and colleagues to write:

> 'If you see Mr. Wood [from work], tell him I am awaiting a letter from him.'

Almost as a postscript Jim remembered to ask:

> 'I hope you have received the brooches; they are not extra good but I think that you will like them.'

As was his way, Jim had found the time and money to send a few trinkets to his beloved family!

PICTURE POSTCARD 3

[Undated. Written to Bertha and the girls, showing four views of Masham in Yorkshire and headed as for letter 2.]

> 'Dear Bertha, just a PC from Masham. We are camping there for a day or two. Hope you and the kiddies are well; I am in the pink. Will write a letter as soon as possible.'

This brief message indicates that Jim's ('D') company had been on the move, acclimatising the men to life under canvas. Several months on from then, it is a safe bet that many of those who were undoubtedly grumbling about camping in Yorkshire would readily offer almost anything to swap their wet, muddy dugout on the front line for the relative comfort of a canvas tent in a dry English field!

Jim Elwell – photograph taken in Richmond, Yorkshire.

POSTCARD 4

[Tuesday, 19 September 1916. Written to Bertha and the girls and headed, 'Pte IJ Elwell, 2607, 'D' Coy, Hut 64, 5th Reserve South Staffs, Scotton Camp, Catterick, Yorkshire.']

This humble, plain blue postcard suggests that significant changes had taken place in Jim Elwell's army life. Eleven weeks on from the previous dated postcard, Jim was still at Scotton Camp and still with the South Staffordshire but he had been transferred to the 5th Reserve Battalion; moreover, his regimental number had been changed from '5937' to '2607'. Quite likely this was a prelude to his shipping out to France; it might simply have been coincidence but whatever the truth, Jim's next letter would carry in its address at the top, 'B.E.F. [British Expeditionary Force], France.'

Most of his final communication from home soil was concerned with the mundane reality of a Tommy's everyday life – shaving correctly and to the sergeant's satisfaction:

'Just a PC to let you know I am well. I want you to try to get me some blades for my razor.....like those I bought at Brum[8]. They are called Gillette Blades, they are the best. I should get about three or four and send them on. I can shave myself a treat with them – they are better than the other razors. I shave in half the time. With love to you and the children, Jim.'

Perhaps Mr. Gillette should have rewarded Jim for such an unequivocally glowing tribute! Yet for Jim, it was simple, common sense – you had to shave properly every day, so get the blades that do the job most effectively. A good, soldier's philosophy – do the necessary well and keep out of trouble!

Nevertheless, shaving was soon to become a relatively minor problem in Private Elwell's daily routine – evidently the South Staffordshire had a ferry ticket for Jim and his mates, and 'Old Fritz', as Jim

A silk embroidered card dedicated to Jim's South Staffordshire Regiment. Such cards were popular with families left at home.

would come to know him, was far from finished. If training at Catterick had been a shock to the system of civilians unversed in the ways of the army, then the Western Front was to prove a living nightmare.

---

[8] The diminutive of 'Brummagem' (derived from the Tudor form, 'Bremwchem') the local name for Birmingham.

CHAPTER THREE

'Into the firing line...'

LETTER 5

[Tuesday 10 October 1916. Written to Bertha and the girls. Headed, '1/6th Battalion South Staffordshire, 9th JBD S24, c/o Army Post Office, British Expeditionary Force, France.']

Sometime between 20th September and 27th September 1916, Jim and a draft of lads who had trained together at Scotton Camp were shipped across to France to join 1/6th Battalion of the South Staffordshire, then based near Bailleulmont on the Somme (see the photograph below of the village). This location lay a few miles to the north of Gommecourt where the battalion, as part of 46th '1st North Midland' Division, had taken part in a diversionary attack on 1st July 1916 – the first day of the Somme campaign. Despite their heavy losses, 2,455 men killed or wounded, the division was deemed to have failed badly in its task and was summarily dismissed from the line; its commander, Major-General the Hon. E.J.M. Stuart-Wortley', had been sent home to England. Engaged in the ensuing, drawn-out Somme campaign 1/6th South Staffordshire, between 1st July and 19th October 1916, had subsequently lost 102 men killed and many more wounded, injured or ill, so drafts of replacements fresh from training in England were gratefully received.

Bailleulmont.

At the time of Jim's arrival at 1/6th South Staffordshire in the village of Bailleulmont, on the northern extremity of the Somme sector, the battalion

was involved in the following pattern of deployment. Paired with 1/5th South Staffordshire[1], 1/6th Battalion was in Divisional Reserve from 17th to 21st September, after which it relieved 1/5th Battalion in the trenches at Berles-au-Bois from 21st to 27th September. Following a very quiet spell in the front line, the battalion went into Brigade Reserve at Berles until 3rd October. (The photograph below shows the village in 1915; by September 1916, when Jim arrived, it had been almost flattened). Writing his last letter in England on 19th

Berles-au-Bois.

September, Jim could not possibly have travelled by train from Catterick to a south coast ferry port, crossed the Channel and entrained to the Somme in less than five days, thus the best guess for the actual date of his arrival with the battalion is 25th September. However, his posting to 1/6th South Staffordshire was to be but a very brief one.

Jim had evidently undergone a few 'repairs' before leaving Catterick, in particular losing a few teeth to the army dentist:

> 'My face is better now, Bertha, but I haven't had any more teeth put in for those they pulled out but still I am well and strong and that's something to be thankful for.'

The short notice of being warned for overseas service and the days travelling had disrupted the steady flow both of letters and parcels from home to Jim, though he had found some compensations in the army's weekly supply of cigarettes and tobacco:

---

[1] 'Paired' means that one of the two named battalions would be in the front line trenches while the other would be in support or reserve, just back from the front line.

'Very pleased to receive your letter...(I had been) anxious to get one...haven't had one for nearly a fortnight.

'I should have liked to get the cake and other things you sent me before I left Scotton but I left word with Harry to send them back. You can send me as much chocolate as you like, I can always eat that. And the tobacco, we have some given to us every Friday and fags for those who don't smoke a pipe. Dear Bertha, I will get you some of those cards as you ask for. You can send a postal order any time – I think I can change them alright.'

The rest of this letter is concerned with the fortunes of family and friends. The reference to Jim's brother, Ted, is intriguing; although younger than Jim, he was already in the army as single men were taken in advance of their married counterparts:

'Is Ted getting better?' [Probably a reference to illness, wound or injury].

'If you see Mr. Wood [a former work colleague of Jim's at S.B. Jagger] tell him I will write to him as soon as I get a chance.

'Thank the little 'uns [his daughters, Lizzie and Lucy] for their cards [see pages 77-78] and you too – it shows you didn't forget my birthday [3rd October 1916, Jim's 37th birthday].

Lucy, Bertha, Jim and Lizzie.

'I think, Bertha, you are having that photo framed... but I don't think I should have troubled... it all costs you money.' [This refers to one of the family photographs, shown above, taken in Walsall during the autumn of 1916.]

'Please don't forget the razor blades.'

These final two comments are typical of matters that were at the forefront of Jim's mind while he was in France – Bertha's shortage of disposable income and the necessities of everyday life as a soldier.

LETTER 6
[Sunday 15 October 1916. Written to Bertha and the girls.]

This letter was written on headed notepaper showing a kilted Scots piper (above) and inscribed:

> 'Bravo Scots, they have done well;
> And charged without a pause;
> Glory be to the righteous;
> You've fought a "freedom" cause.'

> 'The "Contemptible Little Army";
> Is at it now, "full glee!";
> But what of you, Wilhelm the Second;
> When it does get hold of thee?'

Although this letter bore no address, it seems very likely that by the time of its writing Jim had been transferred to 7th Battalion, the Suffolk Regiment, a posting that could not have occurred before 10th October 1916 as Jim wrote home from 1/6th South Staffordshire on that date. Graeme Clarke points out, in a monumental, unpublished work on Walsall servicemen killed in the Great War, that five Walsall lads[2] who trained with the South Staffordshire at Scotton were killed on 28th April at Arras with 7th Suffolk. Jim Elwell was one; another of them, Lance-Corporal Albert Stych M.M., had definitely been transferred to 7th Suffolk on 29th September, and though it is logical that a full draft of Staffordshire men would have been transferred together (the army preferred things to be 'tidy'!), Jim did not transfer until at least the second week of October.

7th Suffolk was one of the four battalions of 35th Brigade and when in the line was usually paired with 7th Norfolk; 35th Brigade was one of the three brigades

[2] The five were:- Jim Elwell, Albert Stych, Arthur Ross, John Dickinson and Harry Birch – for details see page 71. At least two more Scotton men joined 7/Suffolk – Frank Townrow was killed on 15th March 1917 and another, unnamed, man was badly wounded on the same date [see pages 59-60 for letter 42, dated 19th March 1917].

that comprised 12th 'Eastern' Division, a division that was composed entirely of Lord Kitchener's 'New Army' battalions. The division had been in France since June 1915 and had taken part in the Battle of Loos and in the subsequent actions of the Hulluch Quarries, both in October 1915. During March of 1916 the division had been involved in the engagements at the Hohenzollern Craters (near Loos), then in the summer had been heavily involved on the Somme, principally in the Battle of Albert (2nd to 8th July) and in the Battle of Pozières (28th July to 13th August). At the time that Jim Elwell was transferred to 7th Suffolk, the battalion was heavily involved in the Battle of Le Transloy Ridges (1st to 18th October). The reason for the transfer of Jim and a good few of his mates from the South Staffordshire and other battalions was simple – 7th Suffolk had suffered crippling casualties in its earlier actions on the Somme. Since 2nd July, the battalion had lost 259 men killed and many more wounded (306 in the 3rd July attack on Ovillers alone) from a unit strength that had already been well below the establishment level of 1,000 – a regiment that had originally recruited from the east of England now gratefully took any replacement drafts that it could lay hands on and so Jim began to accustom himself to the soft burr of East Anglia.

When Jim arrived at his new battalion, 7th Suffolk had recently returned, on 27th September, from a five-week tour of duty in the Arras sector. On 2nd October, the battalion had moved into the reserve trenches at Bernafay Wood on the Somme and eight days later had moved into the front line trenches near Flers – if Jim joined the Suffolks before 19th October, he was about to experience, and be lucky to survive, a brief baptism of fire in the Battle of Le Transloy Ridges. The Battalion War Diary of 12th October reads:

MAP TWO   The Western Front, 1916-1917

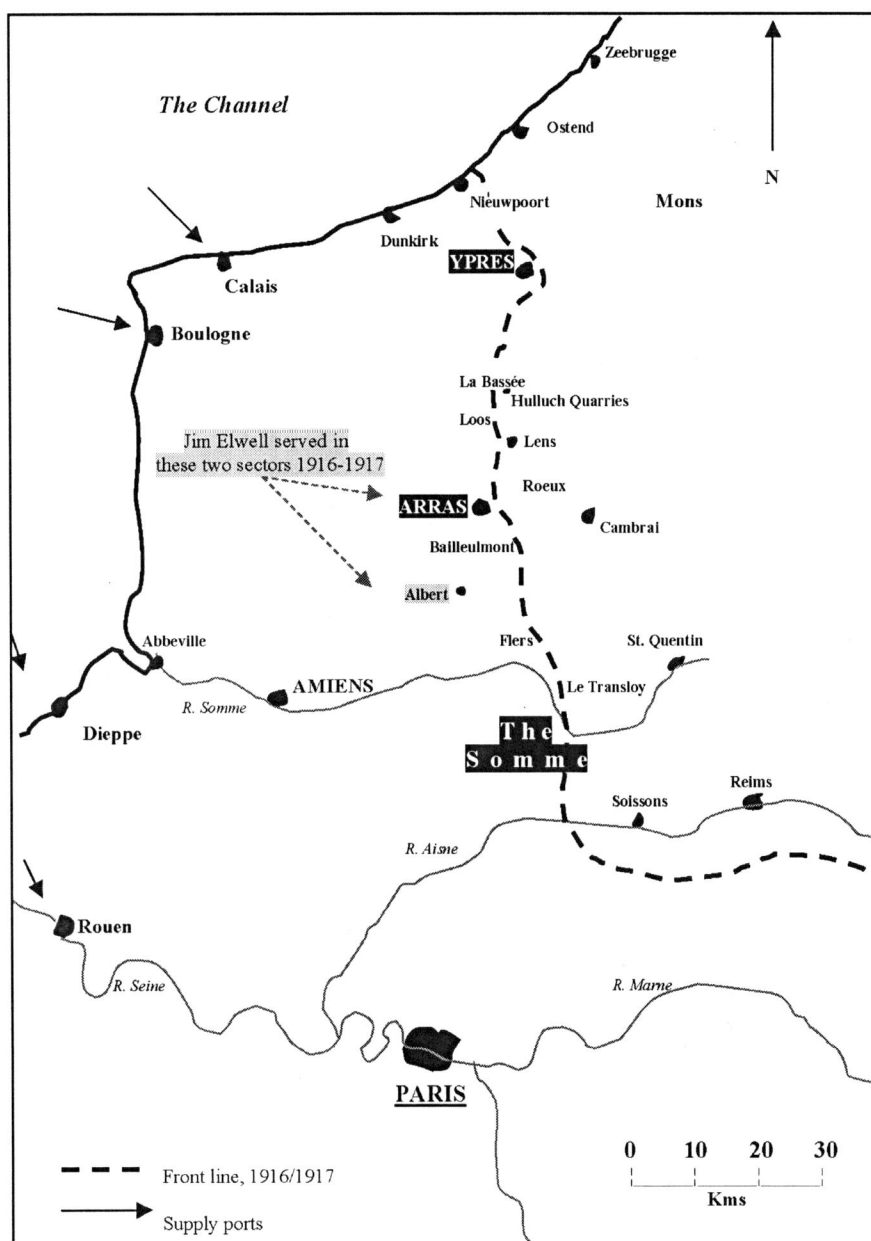

The Channel

Zeebrugge
Ostend
Nieuwpoort   Mons
Dunkirk
YPRES
Calais   N
Boulogne
                    La Bassée
                    Hulluch Quarries
                    Loos
Jim Elwell served in   Lens
these two sectors 1916-1917
                    Roeux
ARRAS
                    Cambrai
Bailleulmont
Albert

Abbeville   Flers   St. Quentin
            AMIENS   Le Transloy
R. Somme
            The
Dieppe   Somme
                    Reims
                Soissons
R. Aisne

Rouen

R. Seine   R. Marne

PARIS   0   10   20   30

– – – Front line, 1916/1917   Kms

→ Supply ports

'With 7/Norfolk and from positions in the sunken road leading to Gueudecourt Wood, the battalion made an assault on Bayonet Trench; advanced at 2 p.m. under heavy crossfire; held up near the German trenches by machine-guns and wire; forced to take cover in shell-holes. Lieutenant-Colonel Murphy [C.O. 7th Suffolk] noted acts of "remarkable bravery" at that point. Withdrew into reserve with over 500 casualties.'

During the course of 13th and 14th October the battalion, '....rested and reformed in Flers Trench', then on 15th the badly-mauled Suffolks moved up to, '....relieve 5/Royal Berkshire in support in Bulls Run³'; over the next two days the men provided, '....(working) parties to

³ This is a trench name.

engage in carrying up water and bombs[4].' Finally, on 19th October the battalion was, *'....relieved by 16/Middlesex [of 29th Division] and went to camp in Mametz Wood – arrived 6pm.'*

Letter Six itself was actually relatively short, probably written in snatched moments in the support lines, and largely concerned with matters at home in Walsall:

'Did you receive the cards[5] I sent you? I am sorry I shan't be able to get any more, not here anyway. I will write for my under-shirt and some top-socks, if you can get some, but don't send them till I write for them.'

Jim's request for extra clothing shows that he was rapidly becoming aware of the necessities of trench life. Even so, he was at this time very concerned about his brother Ted and his wife, Nell, Bertha's sister (right):

Ted Elwell and Nell (née Webster).

'I had a letter from our Ted last night and it was rather disappointing too.... Your Nell has given him the cold shoulder.... I consider it a dirty trick after all he has gone through not only for her alone but for others as well – the same as what I am prepared to do now.'

'...all he has gone through...' refers to the fact that Ted had joined the army before Jim and had most certainly been in the thick of things. Now Jim had had his first taste of trench fighting.

Jim was relieved that Bertha's parcel had arrived before the battalion moved up the line and often out of reach of the postal service:

'Just a line to thank you for the parcel (received Sunday)...I am in the pink. The parcel has come...just in time for we are off up the line tonight, Sunday (15th October).

'We are going (now) and Alf is going with me; glad to tell you he's in the pink. If you see my mother, tell her me and Alf Walker (Bertha's cousin who trained with

Jim at Scotton) are going together and he wishes to be remembered to all of them.'

'P.S. Don't send anything on (to me) till I write again.'

The final comment indicates that Jim had no idea how long his unit would be beyond the Army Post Office (or that he would be transferred) and he certainly did not want parcels lying around where they might be 'accidentally' damaged or opened. This letter also sees the first reference to Alf Walker, a Walsall mate and Bertha's cousin who had had been through basic training with Jim and who was also transferred to 7th Suffolk from 1/6th South Staffordshire at the same time as Jim. Alf was to go through most of what Jim experienced and, though they were occasionally separated, as was the army's way, they remained close friends.

LETTER 7
[Monday 23 October 1916. Written to Bertha and the girls.]

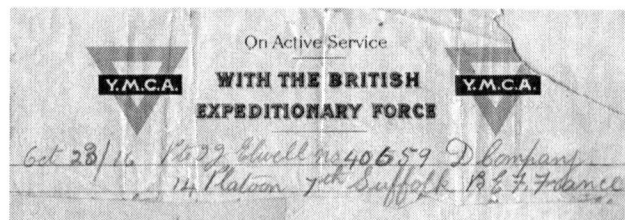

YMCA letterhead: 'On Active Service with the B.E.F.'

This letter, of which but a scrap of the first page remains (above), is written on notepaper headed, *'YMCA, On Active Service With The British Expeditionary Force,'* and carries the address, *'Private I.J. Elwell, 14 Platoon, 'D' Coy, 7th Battalion, Suffolk Regiment, BEF, France.'* [The YMCA provided nearly two hundred centres, in most theatres of war, where soldiers could enjoy refreshments, reading and writing facilities (including free notepaper and envelopes), various entertainments and much-needed rest. These centres were occasionally uncomfortably close to the front line and more than one was destroyed by shellfire; yet for the soldier the YMCA offered a haven of normality in a world seemingly gone mad.]

On 22nd October 7th Suffolk, hard pressed during its three and a half months on the Somme, was transferred to Third Army and at 7 p.m. that day the battalion arrived, in a convoy of motor buses, at Lattre St. Quentin in the Arras sector (see map on page 13). Sadly, it was a sector that Jim would never leave. The men

---

[4] 'Bombs' was the soldiers' name for grenades – a vital ingredient of trench warfare.
[5] These cards are almost certainly the silk embroidered cards that were so popular with the British troops and that Bertha had requested in an earlier letter. See the example on page 24.

moved into billets that were described as '...only fair' and so began three days of, '...rest, cleaning up and training.' The sole existing fragment of this letter relates to Jim's need for 'powder' to make his life more tolerable – whether it was foot powder or 'chat' powder[6] is unclear, as the message shows:

'Dear Bertha, will you get me a tin of powder from Boots cash Chemist – you will know what sort it is as it says on the tin or bottle.'

There is no later reference to suggest whether Bertha's mission was successful!

LETTER 8

[Saturday 28 October 1916. Written to Bertha and the girls. Headed, '14 Platoon, 'D' Coy, 7th Bn, Suffolk Regiment, BEF, France.']

On 26th October, Jim's battalion had, '...proceeded by bus to Arras (from Lattre), relieved 6/DCLI (Duke of Cornwall's Light Infantry). 'C' Company in Achicourt [southern outskirts of Arras]; 'B' Company in Ronville [south eastern outskirts of Arras]; 'A', 'D' [Jim's company] and 'HQ' Companies at Arras. Relief complete by 2:30 am.'[7] Now in reserve, the battalion provided working parties by

The war-damaged town hall at Arras (2).

night, shoring up battered trenches, re-wiring the front line and carrying endless quantities of provisions, materials and equipment to the lads in the firing line – unsurprisingly, this was exhausting and time-consuming work. Although the reserve billets to which they were allocated were in the city of Arras, this did not guarantee their quality:

'I am nearing the firing line. The place we are billeting now is a wreck; it's blown almost to pieces, big shops, warehouses and all other places [see the example, below, of the damaged Town Hall at Arras]. It's all very well to read about it in the papers but you could never realise it unless one saw it and if ever God spares me to come home again I shall have a great deal to tell you, things and sights I shall never forget.'

The proximity of the front line and its dangers turned Jim's mind to those still at home who should have been lending a hand in France:

The people in England don't know there's a war on especially young men that are fit and well enough to fight or they would be out here helping to fight or doing some little bit towards bringing to a close this cruel war. Thank God I am trying to do my little bit in it, live or die. Dear Bertha, I could tell you a lot but I dare not.'

To make matters worse, the postal service in Jim's sector at that time was not all that it might be:

'I haven't received the fags yet...nor your parcel and I am rather sorry you sent that postal order to me because I cannot change it.

'I forgot to ask you, have you received the rosary beads alright? I thought it would be easy to get them here but I find it is very difficult. I should like to get the children some and if I can, they shall have them.'

Even though he was so close to the front line, Jim still had time for his friends and relatives back home:

'How's young Sid [Powell], has he gone yet and how is big Sid [Powell], Maria [Powell], Fred and Teresa [Powell] (shown on page 30 in older age), your mother and all the rest – there are a little too many to mention all the names but when I say all I mean all.

'Please ask Jim to thank all my old friends at Day Street for me and tell him to save a little drop of B-ds [unclear] best – you can't get that sort out here.

'How are my little'uns? Are they good children? Now tell them they must be good little girls for their daddy and pray for him to come home again to you and them.

'I thought it would be easy to get them (cards) but I find it's very difficult. I should like to get the children some – if I can, they shall have them.'

---

[6] 'Chats' were body lice and their eggs; no front line soldier could avoid them and the itching they caused drove men to distraction [see letter 14 on pages 34-35]. The present term, 'chatting', derives from the conversations men had while involved in the communal 'sport' of louse killing.
[7] Quoted from the 7th Suffolk Battalion War Diary.

Fred and Teresa Powell, Jim's landlords.

Jim also reveals that he was not averse to a night out when the opportunity presented itself, though he makes it clear that local prices would limit such evenings:

'Let me tell you this, me and one of my mates went out, Tuesday night I believe it was, for a drink [while they were out of the line 'at rest' in Lattre St. Quentin]. Well, we called for one bottle of beer, a three half-pint bottle; it was only one and a half francs, that's one shilling and three pence in English money! Other things are just as dear, no matter what it is. A man could spend a fortune in very little time here.'

Jim signed off with his usual:

'May God bless you and keep you all safe and bring me back home to you again.'

FIELD SERVICE POSTCARD 9

[Saturday 4 November 1916 Written to Bertha and the girls]

Despite the fact that the field service postcard was extremely brief, even terse, it gave the soldier the chance to let everyone back home know he was alright at a time when he was unable to write a proper letter (see the example, right):

'I am quite well. Letter follows at first oppor- tunity. I have received no letter from you lately.'

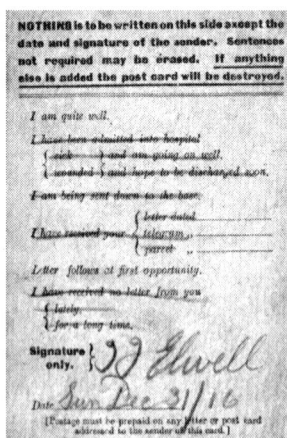

A typical field service postcard. This one was written by Jim on the final day of 1916.

LETTER 10

[Saturday 4 November 1916. Written to Bertha and the girls. Headed, '14 Platoon, 'D' Coy, 7th Bn, Suffolk Regiment, BEF, France.']

Jim begins, as usual, by putting his wife's mind at rest:

'I am in the best of health.'

Yet from 30th October to 2nd November, 7th Suffolk had been in the trenches, relieving 7th Norfolk in the front line, though apart from, '...a few 77mm shells on Hope Street [a trench name[8]],' the four-day tour was very quiet. The typical British trench system consisted of three lines of trenches – firing line, close support and reserve – all connected by narrow communication trenches that were zig-zagged to prevent enfilading fire[9] from the German trenches. The main trenches themselves were divided into short bays known as traverses, each separated from the next by two reversed ninety-degree corners in order to reduce the effects of shell blast. The firing line trench would be dug eight or so feet deep[10] with a notch or fire-step cut into the front edge while the top of the trench, known as the parapet, was reinforced by sandbags. A man might obtain a view towards the enemy lines by using a rudimentary periscope but otherwise he might spend months without actually seeing a German soldier. The rear edge of the trench, known as the parados, was also reinforced with sandbags while the bottom of the trench was usually covered by a wooden duckboard walkway to reduce the strength-sapping effects of mud and water, though nature often won this particular battle. By far the worst aspect of trench life was the weather, as Jim's letter testified:

'I am glad to tell you, Bertha, that I have just come out of the trenches or rather yesterday (Friday). We were in for nearly five days. We are both alright, me and Alf Walker. The weather was very bad while we were there – it rained nearly all the time we were in, but never mind, I came out safe.'

Relieved by 7th Norfolk, the battalion moved into reserve on 3rd November and went into billets at Arras but 'reserve' meant the dreaded working parties at night:

---

[8] On trench maps, individual trenches were known by full grid references but sometimes shortened to the likes of, 'H1 sub-sector'; to the ordinary soldier they were known by names usually given them by the first units to be deployed into those trenches, often reflecting the origin of the unit, (e.g. a London battalion dubbed one trench 'Oxford Street'), or the Tommies' humour, (e.g. 'Ale Trench' and 'Beer Alley.')
[9] That is, firing down the length of a trench and thus causing substantial casualties.
[10] This was the norm except where the water table was high causing diggings to rapidly flood; in such locations, especially much of the Ypres Salient, digging would be shallow and the parapet built up by means of sandbags, timber and earth.

'We are at our own billets now, having a rest but I can tell you we work harder while we are out than when we are in. I would rather be in (the firing line), only for the risk you run.'

During the quiet moments when Jim managed to write this letter, he reflected on everyday life in the firing trenches:

'I should like to tell you what it is like in the firing line but can't, but I can tell you this, there's plenty of rats and plenty of chats, as we call them; you don't have to be long in the trenches before you get crummy[11] – we can't help it if we have to find room for them – but then all the while we were in (the line) we didn't get a wash, a shave or nothing else. Dear Bertha, we are at one of the quietest places on the front. At least they tell us that – I can tell you this, if this is one of the quietest it must be hot in other places! It's very nice to be here – bullets and other little things whizzing over your head and all around you. I wish 'Old Fritz', as we call him, would be more careful when he knows how awkward he is!'

'Rats...and...chats' were the bane of the front line soldier's life. Men often spoke of, 'rats as big as cats' and this reflects how well-fed the rodents were – they had become expert at stealing food and when that failed the rats could always gorge themselves on the never-ending supply of human corpses. Ratting or rat-hunts gave occasionally bored soldiers the chance of a bit of competitive fun and briefly reduced the numbers of the vicious creatures. 'Chats' were body lice and in the trenches no man, whatever his rank, was long free of them. Their tiny eggs hatched in the warm seams of a soldier's clothing and the resultant itching drove men to the edge of despair. In quiet times, men would sit together running fingers or, at some risk, a lighted match along the seams of clothing in a vain attempt to remove some of the infuriating lice and their eggs – the process of searching out and destroying the 'chats' while the men talked and joked became known as 'chatting', a term that is in common usage even today.

Yet again the good and bad points of the postal service were making themselves felt:

'Dear Bertha, I am very sorry to tell you that I haven't had a letter from you for nearly a fortnight, or a parcel. The last I had was about October 24th (nearly a fortnight previously).'

'Dear Bertha, I haven't got time to write to mother yet, so you can let her know I am in the best and hope they all are back home. I have sent a field card to let them know I am well and safe but...before you get this letter I shall be in (the trenches) again.'

This letter, begun on the Saturday, was completed on Sunday and this set Jim to reflecting upon the Sunday routine at home:

'It is now Sunday morning, Bertha, I am sitting having my breakfast alongside Alf Walker – I started this letter last night but I hadn't time to finish it.

'I wish I was having my Sunday breakfast at home. About this time I should be getting ready for Church – I haven't been for weeks, I wish I could. They had Church for the Church of England chaps before we went in the trenches but I didn't go – I wanted to go to my own, else none at all. I must come to a close as I have to go on parade at 8:45 and I haven't a lot of time.'

Jim signed off in his usual manner:

'Remember me to all my friends and may God bless you and the kiddies.'

LETTER 11
[Monday 6 November 1916. Written to Bertha and the girls. Headed, '14 Platoon, 'D' Coy, 7th Bn, Suffolk Regiment, BEF, France.']

After Jim's usual, 'I am in the pink', he reveals the emotion that has nagged away at him since his initial departure for Scotton Camp in June 1916:

'This, Bertha old girl, is always the most touching part of my letters, when I mention you and my children. I can't help it, Bertha, but a lump seems to come up into my throat which oft times is very hard to swallow and very often a tear drops on my paper as I am writing but I hope, please God, it won't be for much longer, for it's cruel.'

'Many a time I have said, especially when it's (Saturday) night, here I am parading about the streets of France while my wife is perhaps doing her marketing and my place should be at her side. Then is the time we think of home, when a thought crosses our mind of the past, then is the time we think of home. I wish, Bertha,

Fred Powell's foundry in Blue Lane West.

I was again having a spin in Fred Powell's motor car[12]; but never mind, tell him to save a little drop of petrol and perhaps one of these days I shall be coming – God grant it be soon.

'Keep up your spirits, Bertha my girl, and pray that God will bless me with that good fortune; and yet, Bertha, if you could only see you would think it impossible for any man to come safe through it. Now, Bertha, don't be downhearted, trust to God and wait, pal, wait.

'Are my little ones alright and are they good girls? Tell them their daddy sends his best love to them both. God bless them both and you too.'

Just as quickly, as if to hold his feelings in check, Jim turns to the more 'mundane' matters of life in the trenches. He writes especially of the lottery of front line or reserve and the soldier's ability to sleep whenever the opportunity occurs:

'Dear Bertha, let me tell you how I fared when I was in the trenches. I didn't go in the reserve line at all – I went right up into the first line. I was one of the first two on sentry, along with a chap named Gibbs. They are all strangers to us (in the new battalion); you see, there is only about seven of the old chaps[13] in this company and Alf is one of them and these chaps are, as I say, strangers to us all but the chap as I was on with was a decent sort – he has been in the trenches before and we were alright together. You soon get used to one another, just the same as if we had been together for years. Alf (Walker, seen with Jim, right) seemed to be more fortunate than me – he was in the reserve line all the while; we went in (Monday) morning and came out (Friday) dinner time. It seems very strange – I was the first to go on sentry and the last to be relieved. I can tell you, Bertha, it's rotten to be there to hear the shots and

Jim (left) with Alf Walker at Scotton.

shells come flying all around you – it makes you keep your eyes open, I can tell you. And sleep, you have to get that when you can – when I get the chance, shots nor shells don't worry me (as) I am soon in Dreamland. Well, in fact, a soldier can sleep anywhere or anyhow, on sandbags, in dugouts or what-not – it matters not to Tommy Atkins[14], he's very glad to get the opportunity.'

Towards the end of his letter, Jim mentions something he has heard from his brother Ted and that has been worrying him:

'Ted and Nell are not getting on too well...it's nothing to do with me – they will settle it best themselves, the same as we have done before. What do you say, old girl?'

LETTER 12

[Wednesday 8 November 1916. Written to Bertha and the girls on notepaper decorated with violets. Headed, '14 Platoon, 'D' Coy, 7th Bn, Suffolk Regiment, BEF, France.']

---

[12] Fred Powell must have been relatively well off as motor cars were not common possessions in 1917. He owned at least two houses, including the one in which Jim and Bertha lived, and a small foundry (shown on this page) at the back of 41, Blue Lane West.

[13] A reference to the lads who transferred from 1/6th South Staffordshire back in September 1916 – they had evidently been divided among the four rifle companies of 7th Suffolk.

[14] 'Thomas Atkins' or 'Tommy Atkins' was a name coined in the 19th Century by the Duke of Wellington for the ordinary soldier when asked for a name to write onto a sample paybook.

On Monday, 7th November 1916, the battalion relieved 7th Norfolk and commenced a four-day tour of duty in the front line:

'I am writing this letter, Bertha, in the trenches, we came in yesterday [this phrase is deleted, probably by the Censor's pencil]. I have just come into my dugout for a little rest – we don't get a lot, you know, so when we get the chance to rest we make the best of it.

'Let me tell you that we are having very bad weather while we are in the trenches, raining more or less all the while and cold with it but I hope by the time you get this letter I shall be out again having a rest. Well I mean we do get a bed to have a good sleep on, what we don't get here.

'You ask about Alf (Walker), well he's alright; we are together and all OK so don't you worry and keep on hoping.

'Bertha, send what you think will keep me free from those 'chats', as we call them, and I'll see that I use it.'

The rain and cold mentioned by Jim was the forerunner of what was to be one of the worst winters in living memory. The inclement weather was made to feel worse by the lack of contact with home:

'Dear Bertha, sorry to tell you I haven't received the fags that were sent me – I wished I had for I am smoking a lot of fags now[15].

'This is the first letter I have received from you for two weeks – they have all got lost, I think. It was about the 22nd or 23rd October I sent those beads – they were white ones, nice beads. I am sorry you haven't got them safely.

'Please don't send me any money if you are given any to send – buy some chocolate with it or something else. Postal orders are no good (as) I can't change them.

'I have written a letter to my mother but haven't sent it yet – I wrote it two days ago, before we came in the trenches but when we move it's awkward to get them away.'

In Jim's absence from home there had evidently been an addition to the wider family but again it merely served to emphasise to him just how far away from home he was:

'Dear Bertha, I hope your MaryAnn's [Jim Powell's wife] going on alright with the big daughter [Teresa] as

MaryAnn and Jim's niece, baby Teresa Powell.

you call her – I wish I was at home so that I could have a look at her but never mind, I keep on hoping and trusting to God that I shall soon be home again.' (MaryAnn and baby Teresa are pictured left).

Ever the family man, at the end of his letter Jim was already thinking of still-distant Christmas:

'Good night and God bless you all.
'P.S. Tell Lizzie and Lucy they can send me chocolate for Xmas.'

LETTER 13

[Thursday 9 November 1916. Written to Bertha and the girls. Headed, '14 Platoon, 'D' Coy, 7th Bn, Suffolk Regiment, BEF, France.']

This letter was written in the middle of a fairly quiet spell in the trenches, though later that day (9th November) German trench mortars caused a few problems for the company on Jim's right when a trench was blown in:

'I am writing this in my little dugout. The weather here this morning is much better than usual for it has been rotten. It makes one feel a little more cheerful when the weather is bright.

'I hope I get the parcel you have sent....I am wanting a little parcel, I don't care what it is so long as I get one. I want to be like Alf Walker – he wrote and told his sister to send him a little parcel as often as she could. He is going on alright, well in fact we are both in the pink. I have just seen him; he is on a different duty to me again. I am again on sentry duty; each time I have been in (the trenches) I have touched for that and Alf is doing work duty but we shall be together when we go out again.'

'Dear Bertha, you speak of something for the chest – I don't know if I should be allowed to wear it so I don't

[15] Cigarettes were among the few comforts that the front line soldier could depend upon.

33

think I should waste your money on that, if I was you. Thank our Sid [Powell] for his offer – he's a good old sport and always was, God bless him. Tell him I am coming one of these days to punch that sand about for him [Sid was an iron-caster by trade] but let me tell you, Bertha, all I want is something to keep me warm while the cold weather is on.'

Most of the letter is concerned with life at home for Jim's family, especially his girls, and friends:

'Dear Bertha, tell my little ones to say that prayer every day and night for their daddy to come home safe again and I am sure God will answer their prayer. Give my love to them and say their daddy is alright.'

'Sorry you didn't get the beads – they were such nice ones. I sent your mother a card – did she get that? And how is she going on?'

Because danger stared Jim in the face, he was constantly hoping that others would be spared the same, particularly his brother Ted who had joined the army before him:

'I am glad to hear Ted and Nell are alright – has he come home for good? I hope he has. Please tell me about him in your next letter.

Jim (left) with Will Simpson.

'Glad to hear that young Sid [Powell] is not going yet and by the by, has our Will [Simpson, Jim's brother-in-law, married to Nell – see photograph above] gone yet or Tom [Spencer, Jim's brother-in-law, married to Rose]? I am sending them both a field card today.'

The end to Jim's letter is typical of him, a mixture of the practical and the emotional:

'Please remember me to all I know.'
'P.S. Bertha, will you send me two more blades. (Also) I am sorry to hear of Mr. Stringer's son – I hope he will soon get better.'

'God bless you all and keep you safe till I come home again.
xxxxxxx Share these kisses.'

LETTER 14

[Sunday 12 November 1916.
Written to Bertha and the girls.]

At the time of writing this letter, Jim's battalion was in reserve and his 'D' Company billeted in Arras; at night they were, as usual, assigned to the perennial, strength-sapping working parties:

'I came out of the trenches last night but I was too tired to write; I started to write but I fell asleep writing so I had to give it up.

'Just a line or two in answer to your kind and welcome letter. I had two just as I came out of the trenches. We had a lot better weather this time, it was cold but nice and dry. It rained more or less all the time we were in the last time but let me tell you I have come out safe once again and so has Alf. We are both in the best of health and I hope you and the children are as well.'

'Dear Bertha, I wish I had got that powder now for I am all alive with livestock and they don't half bite; they have made blisters on me as big as walnuts. They do itch, in fact I scratched myself until I have made myself bleed – my body is covered with blisters that smart; they are cruel – I am rubbing and scratching myself all the while, I do wish that parcel would come as I could put some of that stuff on me before I went into the trenches again. Every man is the same and I can't help it.'

Jim's torment from the chats was par for the course, especially while in the front line, as soldiers rarely had the chance to wash themselves and certainly not to change their clothes. To make matters worse, when the blisters burst from the persistent scratching, there was every likelihood of infection setting in as dirt was an ever-present part of a soldier's existence. Not only was Jim's body taking a battering but also the normal confidence imparted by his strong faith:

'I forgot to tell you I lost the crucifix off those beads Father Roskell gave me – I can't find it anywhere. I am vexed about it because you know I honour and respect the one who gave them to me [Fr. Roskell was the priest who married Jim and Bertha in September 1908]. Bertha, remember me to Father McDonell and Father Clavin and to all those men at the Church.'

By now Jim was beginning to feel very frustrated with the postal service's infrequent parcel deliveries to him in France and also the poor return service to home:

'I haven't had either of the parcels yet, the one Jim sent me nor the one you sent. I have had only one parcel since I have been in France and that was the one I had before I left the base, When you send one again, put the address well in one or two places – there are several chaps that have had parcels sent them and they have got lost.'

'I can't understand how the beads have got lost; Alf has sent some home and they have had those alright. Mine were beauties; if I see any more I shall have them if it costs me the last franc I have.'

He might have been many miles away but Jim's mind was forever dwelling on the difficulties he suspected his wife was experiencing back in Walsall:

'I suppose by now you are getting a bit settled down on your own but I dare say you have a lot to do. How do you manage with the kiddies? Does Maria [Powell] have them till you get home and are they good little children? Tell them that their daddy sends his best love to them both and tell them that I say they must be good children for their mother.'

As ever, Jim wanted to keep in close touch with what was happening to his former workmates, not least his former employer's son who apparently had been called up by the army:

'If you go to the shop remember me to them all. How's Mr. Wood getting on without SBJ [S.B. Jagger, Jim's employer's son]? Where has he gone to and how's he getting on with army life? He will find it a bit different to sitting in his office and running about up and down stairs. How are Emmie and all the girls?'

Jim's time in the trenches had seemingly strengthened his faith and his letters now often came to their conclusion with a prayer:

'Oh clement, oh loving sweet Virgin Mary, pray for my wife and my children that God in his mercy will keep them safe and take me back home to them once again. Pray to God that this terrible war will soon come to an end.
xxxxxxx Share them among you.'

LETTER 15
[Thursday 16 November 1916. Written to Bertha and the girls.]

He doesn't mention it in his letter but Jim's battalion was at that time on the second day of another relatively quiet tour of duty in the trenches, although the following day witnessed a 'whizz-bang' attack [so called on account of the low trajectory, sharp sound and consequent very short warning they afforded troops] on the company to the right of 'D' Company, killing one man and wounding three. His tour in the firing line must have been cold and wet as his hands were in poor condition and he was suffering from a cold but it did not stop him thinking of his mates back home:

'I have got a little bit of a cold but it will soon wear off.'

'Dear Bertha, don't think I am asking too much of you but I wish I had got a pair of mittens – the back of my hands are all chapped very badly and if I had a pair of those I think it would protect them a lot. Thank Lizzie [his sister] for the helmet (probably a Balaclava) – it's a very good one.
'Tell (Fred) his parcel of fags…. has gone west. But we have plenty of fags issued to us in the Army – well in fact I have never been short of them yet; and tobacco, too.
'Thank our young Sid for the few lines he wrote to me. Tell him to buck up and get strong (for) he will want it all when he is out in France.'

At long last parcels began to arrive for Jim and the change in his spirits is apparent although the errant beads he sent home were still a source of frustration:

'I received your parcel last Tuesday…thanks very much for the good things you put in it. You didn't put any money in it, did you? Everything that was in was in good condition bar the biscuits and of course they were in bits. But I enjoyed them and the chocolate – I like chocolate and can do with as much as you can afford to send me.
'I forgot to tell you, I have had a parcel from my mother too.
'Have you received those beads yet that I sent for my little ones? Tell the kiddies I will send them something if possible for their Christmas box – I have seen something I should like for them. Have you heard of your beads yet? I am sorry they have got lost but never mind, I have another set for you.'

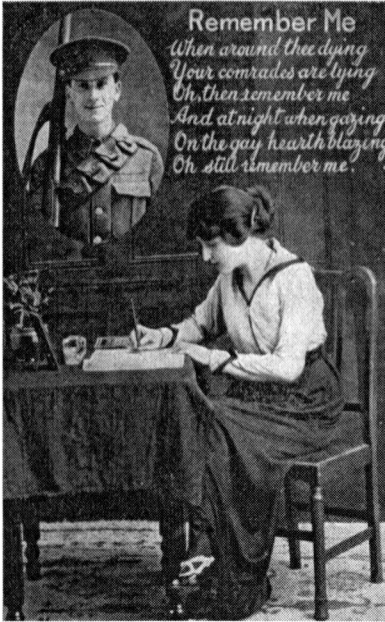

The all-important postcard... The postcard was probably the most valuable link between the front-line soldier and his friends and relatives back home. Cards varied from the simple, plain postcard to the cartoon style cards depicting caricatures of the Tommy's way of life. As the war progressed, so the range of cards increased, with the French and Belgian civilians seeing an opportunity to make a few francs. Postcards showing the places where the British soldiers were fighting were popular, as were the cards that detailed the damage that had been done to many of the towns and cities along the Western Front – it was a way of showing the folks back home where a man was serving without upsetting the dreaded censor. For the Tommy who had a few extra francs to spend there were colourful, silk-embroidered cards that were much in demand back in England. Finally, there were the so-called 'sweetheart' cards (depicted here) whose sentiments now appear rather cloying but which were remarkably popular at the time.

Jim's chirpiness carried over into his enquiries about the folks at home:

'Well, Bertha, how are they all going on in the old town? Is there plenty of work about now? And how are all my mates at the shop?

'Are Fred and Teresa alright? Tell Fred I am coming one of these (Sundays) to have a ride in his motor with him.' [Apart from being related to Jim by marriage, his landlord and next-door neighbour, Fred Powell owned a small foundry at the back of 41, Blue Lane, producing brass and nickel castings for Walsall's celebrated saddlery industry. Thus he was one of the town's renowned craftsmen known as loriners.]

'If you go up to mother's tell her I am sorry to hear of them all being so bad. Tell them to cheer up – it's no use being downhearted, it won't make things any better.'

'Cheer up', and '…it's no use being downhearted', were phrases typical of the men in the trenches who were

more than accustomed to making the best of a bad lot. Jim signed off in his usual manner:

'God bless you all and keep you safe till I come home again.'

xxxxx [Kisses for Bertha, Lizzie and Lucy].

LETTER 16
*[Monday 20 November 1916.
To Bertha and the girls.]*

On Sunday, 19th November, Jim's battalion was, '....relieved by 7/Norfolk. Dispositions as before [namely, 'C' Company in Achicourt, 'B' in Ronville, 'A', 'D' and HQ in Arras]. Relief completed quietly.' Once in reserve, the battalion war diary recorded the ensuing three days as, '....quiet. Working parties.' This duty was universally unpopular with the men as it meant long hours, hard work and little rest. The harsh winter in the trenches was also taking its toll of Jim Elwell – his complaints and minor illnesses were those regularly suffered by many of his comrades in arms:

'I have a bit of a cold on my chest and it's bad in my back – if it doesn't get better soon I shall be compelled to fall sick but I hope it will be (better) by the time you get my letter because it's a thing I hate doing, to fall sick, if I can avoid it any way.'

'What sort of weather are you having in old England? I hope it's much better there than it is here for it's cold and nasty, damp weather, just the sort to give chaps colds. I hope it will soon pick up – I would sooner have it frosty (as) it's healthier and better to get about.'

It is difficult for us of the 21st Century to visualise the plight of the 'other ranks' on a tour of duty in the trenches. A wearying, heavily-laden approach march would bring the company to the narrow communication trench that was often thick with mud, deep in water or frozen solid. Men of the unit being relieved would be struggling in the opposite direction, frequently passing ribald comments towards their relief, safe in the knowledge that they themselves would be 'out of it' for a few short days. In the case of 7th Suffolk, they were taking over a sector with which they were familiar, so they would immediately know the location of the best dugouts or 'funk holes', where the latrines were, which sections of trench were worst for sniper fire and so on. Twice a day, at first light and at dusk, the men would be 'stood to' with full weaponry on the firing step facing the enemy, as these were the most likely times for an attack to come in. Usually all was quiet so most of the men were stood down for breakfast, a meal that might consist of fried bacon, bread and strong sweet tea if they were lucky but more often breakfast was cold, apart from the mandatory brew. The unlucky lads (and Jim seemed to be unluckier than most in this respect) did a stint on 'sentry-go' where they were expected to be alert at all times – falling asleep on guard was, for obvious reasons, considered a very serious offence. Even if there was no organised enemy action, most days witnessed a brief period of 'daily hate' during which the German artillery would lob over a few shells or trench mortar bombs and the British artillery or trench mortar batteries would reply in kind. Then all would usually go quiet for the rest of the day. The sentries would change but most men would settle down to fill the long hours of boredom, reading letters, writing letters, 'chatting' or, in the winter months, more likely trying to keep warm and dry. Keeping warm in the bitter winter of 1916-1917 was nigh on impossible; lucky men might wear fleecy jerkins over their uniform and might have the benefit of woollen gloves or mittens and maybe a Balaclava-style helmet (such as that received by Jim) to help keep out the frost. To combat the rain was even more difficult. All a man could do was to huddle into a small recess in the trench wall, pull his oilskin cape up to his neck and wait for the torrent to cease. When it did, the bottom of the trench was likely awash with water and liquid mud that had nowhere to go but to seep into the men's boots to soak already cold feet; constant exposure to this treatment led to a condition known as 'trench foot', a problem to which Jim was not immune, as his letters will show. Trench foot was so common that each platoon officer was charged with the task of regularly inspecting his men's feet and ensuring that they were treated with evil-smelling but quite effective whale oil; in addition, every man was expected to carry a change of socks, yet these were often as wet as those the man was already wearing. Consequent to these conditions, colds, bronchitis and pneumonia were well known to the trench soldier as was an influenza-like infection known as 'trench fever'.

During the day food was brought up to the front line, hot rations (if the men were fortunate) in large 'dixies', while dry rations were delivered, often mixed together, in sacks. The perennial 'brew', strong and sweet, was the Tommy's mainstay – lack of tea would lead to near-rebellious thoughts! Yet if the food was adequate and

men were with their mates, the 'grousing' was not too serious – it was often said that if a soldier grumbled then there wasn't too much wrong with his morale!

'I am glad to tell you that Alf is well and strong and as jolly as ever – I don't see much of the other (Walsall) chaps (as) they are in a different company.'

The arrival of parcels, usually shared among groups of mates, always managed to cheer up the men:

'I had your parcel safe – the fruit was all good but the biscuits were all smashed up. I ate them anyway and they were very nice and so was the chocolate – it's better stuff than we get here and the price of it here, well it's like buying gold. Dear Bertha, don't send me any gloves, we have just had an issue of them. You can get me the mittens and send them.'

Jim was forever concerned that the little things that he sent home to his family were not making it through the overworked army postal system:

'Did you get those things I sent you and the little'uns….they were very pretty.
      'I want it to be as good and merry a Christmas as we had last year. Let us hope it will be a more merry one next year.'

He signed off in his usual manner:

'God bless you and keep you safe, all of you and bring me back home to you again.'
'PS: tell Jim the fags haven't come yet and remember me to them all.'

LETTER 17

[Friday 15 December 1916. Written to Bertha and the girls.]

For some unknown reason, there was a three-week hiatus between Jim's previous letter and this one, though it is quite possible that letters may have gone astray. During the intervening period the battalion had alternated with 7/Norfolk between reserve and front line trenches on four-day tours of duty. In reserve, the Suffolks had continued to be billeted in Arras, where their time was mainly taken up by the tedious, wearying work parties, though on 30th November they had the opportunity to try out the new, small, box respirator in a tear gas hut, apparently without ill effects. In the line, they operated in the H1 sub-sector in front of Arras where their tours, apart from intermittent trench mortar activity, were remarkably quiet – probably more so than when in reserve where rest was interrupted by work!

On 15th December, the battalion was back in reserve in Arras where again it was eerily quiet, although just a day later three 5.9-inch shells did fall in Rue Pasteur near 7/Suffolk's Battalion Headquarters. Jim was not to know it but this was the last letter that he was to write in reserve or in the line for some ten weeks, though as usual the prospect of

The war-damaged library in Arras.

home leave was out of the question. By now, Jim was beginning to pay the price of regular tours of duty in partially flooded front line trenches, suffering problems with his feet:

'Just a line in answer to your kind and welcome letter. I am better in myself than I have been for a long time, with the exception of my feet that are getting very bad. I am afraid I shall suffer with trench feet but you can't wonder at it. The weather has been so bad this last time that we have been in the trenches in rain and snow and it's very cold. I could not keep my feet warm, try as I might. We came out of the trenches tonight (Thursday) and we had an inspection of our feet as soon as we came out and mine were very bad. I don't know what they will do with me yet but they took my name so I can't tell you anything yet; you will know as soon as I can let you know but perhaps they can get a good deal better while I am out.'

Trench foot was caused by the conjunction of two factors – feet that were constantly soaked in water or liquid mud and persistent low temperatures that led to gradual loss of feeling in the feet. Extreme cases might even result, like frostbite, in the loss of toes but even milder cases were painful and rendered a man unfit for duty. The authorities were so exercised about the problem that at one stage it was considered a self-inflicted problem – an entirely unrealistic view.

'I started this letter last night but I was that tired I had

to leave it so I must finish it today. I have been to the doctor's this morning but my feet feel much better now; it's when I am in the trenches that they are so bad. He stuck a needle in my feet several times and in different places and I could not feel it so you can tell how my feet are numbed with cold. God knows, Bertha, it must be cruel to have frost-bitten feet but I don't want to worry you about that.'

In Bertha's previous letter she had mentioned that Sid Powell (the elder) had suggested that he was prepared to be in the line with Jim – eliciting a considerate but clearly bemused response:

'Thank (Sid) for me for being so good to me and tell him not to even think of being out here. I know he's willing to share my lot with me but if he only knew, he would say Old England's the place for me. I wish I were there, France would never see me again, I tell you!'

As ever, the postal service was both good and bad. Several packages arrived together and part of Jim's reply confirms that his younger brother Ted had most certainly experienced army life before him – but then Ted had been single at that time:

'I have had your letter with the blades in it. I have had two parcels from you, one from mother, one from Lucy and several registered letters; I had three in one day – I thought I was doing great, money and fags galore. Tell Jim I have had his fags. So what Ted tells you about having plenty of fags and tobacco is quite true – you need not send any. Please don't send me any money – I have plenty more than I can spend.'

'Dear Bertha, don't rob yourself for me [Jim was obviously worried that Bertha might be having money problems] and don't send any more fags nor pomade, nor tobacco – we have plenty. I've got no time to smoke tobacco I have that many fags.

'I can understand you when you say the shoes and all other things are so dear but keep on smiling, old girl, and don't worry so much about me – I can tell by your letters that you are doing so.'

In connection with the amount of money that Bertha had available at that time, a letter dated 29th November 1916 (top of page 39) had arrived at Blue Lane West – it did not increase her money but merely confirmed, several weeks after the event, that Jim had been transferred:

Separation Payment Transfer to 7th Suffolk.

'Transfer of Payment of Separation Allowance and Allotment of Pay – to Mrs. B. Elwell, dated 29/11/16. Transfer from 6/South Staffords to 7/Suffolks.'

In the meantime, Jim was concerned about the post from France to home:

One of the silk handkerchiefs that Jim sent home.

'Please tell me if you get the cards and handkerchiefs (above) – I gave them to a chap as was coming home on leave to post for me so he will post them in old England. I hope you will like them.'

Jim signed off with his regular mention of the children:

'I daresay you never get tired of reading my letters – thank my little'uns for the chocolate they are sending me; kiss them for me – I wish I could (kiss them myself). I hope, please God, the time will soon come round for me to do so.'

'My best wishes for a merry Christmas and a happy New Year. God bless you all and keep you safe till I return again.'

During the late afternoon of Monday, 18th December the entire 12th Division was relieved by 14th 'Light' Division, with 7th Suffolk being replaced in reserve by 6th Battalion, the King's Own Yorkshire Light Infantry. The weary troops marched seven miles west out of Arras to billets in the villages of Agnez-lès-Duisans, Gouves and Montenescourt (see map on page 13). By 8 p.m. the changeover was complete. It is highly likely that within minutes of falling out many of the men were fast asleep – it had been a tiring few weeks.

LETTER 18
[Thursday 21 December 1916. Written to Bertha and the girls.]

On Tuesday, 19th December Jim's battalion marched eight miles further west to the village of Ambrines where they moved into the rest billets that they were to occupy for the next six weeks, although the men were not party to such information. The billets that the troops found there were in very poor condition and after an uncomfortable night they spent the following five days cleaning muddied and tarnished equipment and improving the state of the billets; it was hard work but well worth the effort. Jim was able to reflect at leisure on the arrivals in the recent post:

'I have received your parcel that was packed in the wooden box; let me thank you for everything in it – there wasn't a mince pie broken but it came at a very awkward time. We were just leaving our billets for another place where we now are [Ambrines]. We are having a rest, I can't say how long for, I'm sure, but however long it may be it will be very welcome. I am also glad to say I have

Nell Simpson, Jim's sister.

received the parcel from Church – a khaki shirt and a pair of socks. I shan't wear them here; if I can I shall send them home. Will you thank them for me please? Tell them I shall need their prayers but if they pray for me I shall pray for them. God bless them all.

'I have had the mittens with the (religious) medal on and you can tell him (who Jim means is not known) I shall wear it. Don't send me any more tobacco or fags or money, I have plenty. Don't worry so much about me and do try to buck up – if you don't, how do you expect me to? Let my mother know I am well and tell her I am sorry I haven't written. Dear Bertha, I have just received another parcel, I think it is from Lucy [Jim's sister] – that makes three this week.'

'Thank my little'uns for their card and their share in the parcel; kiss them for me and tell them their daddy sends them a good Christmas kiss. By the by, have you had your cards and handkerchiefs yet?'

However, Bertha's most recent letter had carried upsetting news about one of Jim's sisters, Nell (see photo on page 39):

'I am sorry to hear of our Nell having to go in the hospital[16] but I hope, please God, she will soon be better and out again.'

Jim's letter also spoke of contrasting fortunes for two Walsall soldiers:

'I am glad to tell you Alf (Walker) is alright; we are both together. I am sorry to hear that cousin Harry is missing; you said cousin Jim but I think you mean Harry Wassall. Let us hope, please God, he will be found alive.'

Harry Wassall was the son of one of Jim's mother Martha's brothers. He had been born in Birmingham and enlisted in that city in the Royal Warwickshire Regiment during late 1915 or early 1916. His unit, 2/5th (Territorial Force) Battalion, landed in France on 21st May 1916 as part of 61st '2nd South Midland' Division and after an initial period of training was moved into the line to the south of Armentières on the French border to learn the intricacies of trench warfare. It appears that on Sunday, 2nd July 1916 Private Harry Wassall had been on regular trench duty when he was killed in one of the random attacks that contributed to the persistent rise in casualties on the Western Front. He is buried in plot I. H. 2 of Rue du Bacquerot No.1 Military Cemetery, Laventie, Pas de Calais, France. He was the first of the close-knit circle of family and friends to die in the war.

Pte. Harry Wassall – Rue du Bacquerot No.1 Military Cemetery, Laventie.

LETTER 19

[Saturday 23 December 1916. Written to Bertha and the girls.]

These few days, from 20th to 25th December, were possibly the most restful and relaxed of Jim's entire time in the army. Withdrawn from the line into rest, a unit was usually given a bit of leeway for a while before being worked back up to readiness for their return to front line duty. 7th Suffolk's 'leeway' just happened to coincide with Christmas and the men most certainly appreciated their good fortune.

Letter 19 is concerned exclusively with Christmas and is covered in the following chapter.

Out of the line – '...a comfortable bed at last!'

LETTER 20

[Sunday 24 December 1916. Written to Bertha and the girls.]

This is the third letter that Jim wrote to his family in the space of just four days and is testimony to how much he was missing his wife and children at Jim's, *'best time of the year.'* Again, this letter is concerned exclusively with matters relating to Christmas and is dealt with in the following chapter.

Note: 7th Suffolk's officers made an effort to make Christmas Day 1916 seem a bit special for men who had been in and out of the trenches for several months. The

[16] The reason for Nell's hospitalisation is not known.

It looks rather pretty to see a picture of us at dinner in the yard of one of our billets, doesn't it?

Sketches of Tommy's life Up the line – N° 5 — The main duties in the Front Line in the daytime are watching the periscope, and looking up in the air for trench mortars, with a whistle ready to blow for a warning.

Jim Elwell and the 7th Battalion of the Suffolks were fortunate to be away from trench duty for several weeks either side of Christmas 1916 – yet it would be more than repaid in blood in April 1917.

troops had, '...*three good feeds on Christmas Day and.... also had some Christmas pudding.*' They finished up at night with a concert in which Jim was given the opportunity to test his singing voice but he commented, '*I think my voice gets too weak for singing now but anyway I did my best.*' Overall, they had as good a time as was possible under the circumstances. It was in stark contrast to trench life but the memory would soon fade as the serious matter of training for a major offensive took a grip.

CHAPTER FOUR

'We have had ... a decent time this Christmas.'

As will be seen, Christmas was clearly Jim's favourite time of year and to be so far away from his nearest and dearest hit him hard. Christmas was on his mind from early in November and the association of Christmas with children was foremost in his thoughts:

'P.S. Tell Lizzie and Lucy they can send me chocolate for Xmas.'
[8th *November*]

Jim's next tour of duty in the trenches again brought to his mind considerations of Christmas and his children, Lizzie and Lucy:

'Tell the kiddies I will send them something if possible for their Christmas box – I have seen something I should like for them. Have you heard of your beads yet? I am sorry they have got lost but never mind, I have another set for you.'
[16th *November 1916*]

Once again in reserve billets in Arras, Jim remembered Christmas 1915 back in Walsall and though he knew deep down the celebrations would be muted he tried to put on a brave face:

'I want it to be as good and merry a Christmas as we had last year. Let us hope it will be a more merry one.'
[20th *November 1916*]

The ensuing four weeks saw Jim's battalion involved in four-day tours of duty in the trenches then in reserve at Arras. It was a busy time both in and out of the line so Jim had fewer opportunities to write and his next recorded letter is dated 15th December so he seized the chance to pass on his season's greetings:

'My best wishes for a merry Christmas and a happy New Year. God bless you all and keep you safe till I return again.'
[15th *December 1916*]

Three days later, on 18th December, 7th Suffolk was relieved by 6th Battalion, King's Own Yorkshire Light Infantry as 14th 'Light' Division replaced 12th 'Eastern' Division in the central Arras sector. By 8 p.m. the battalion had settled into temporary billets to the west of Arras in the three villages of Agnez-lès-Duisans, Gouves and Montenescourt (see map on page 13). Word spread rapidly along the grapevine that the division was at long last going into rest – and Christmas was just around the corner. There were a lot of happy Tommies that cold winter night! When the battalion was on the road again directly after breakfast on 19th December, a few lads wondered whether the rumours were really true but the doubts were soon dispelled as company after company arrived at more permanent billets in Ambrines, just to the south of the Arras-St. Pol road and well back from the enemy's artillery. The lads didn't know it then but Ambrines was to be their home until 29th January, first at rest then, after Christmas, undergoing intensive training that must surely have put suspicions of a major offensive into the minds of the old hands. A more immediate priority was improving the standard of billets that were referred to in the war diary as, '...*bad*'; the five days up to Christmas Eve were spent in making the living quarters habitable and in cleaning up men, uniforms and equipment. Jim was fortunate in that he received Christmas cards and a parcel from his family just in time for what would pass for festivities in the army.

'Thank my little'uns for their card and their share in the parcel; kiss them for me and tell them their daddy sends them a good Christmas kiss.'
[21st *December 1916*]

'You will find enclosed a card wishing you a merry Christmas and happy New Year – I hope you will like it because it's a [Suffolk] regimental card giving you the places where they have fought in this war.'
[23rd *December*]

The card referred to, enclosed with his letter of 23rd December, was not, as Jim states, a regimental card but in fact a divisional card, produced by 12th 'Eastern'

Division (see below). The front cover shows the divisional emblem, the ace of spades, the years the division had been on the Western Front (1915, 1916, 1917), and its major actions, namely Loos, Hohenzollern Redoubt, Hulluch Quarries and Ovillers (Somme). To

12th 'Eastern' Division greetings card for Christmas 1916 and the New Year of 1917.

the right of the emblem is a soldier in the trenches while to the left is a farmer in front of a haywain, signifying the eastern England origins of the division. At the foot of the cover is the inscription, *'Christmas and New Year Greetings.'* The reverse of the card is a night scene of men in the trenches, with the sky lit by star-shells; at the top of the picture is the ace of spades with a scroll inscribed, *'TWELFTH'*. Inside the card is written:

'FROM Pte I. J. Elwell
To Mrs. I. J. Elwell & Children
CHRISTMAS 1916   NEW YEAR 1917'

Jim was obviously very pleased to receive a parcel at Christmas and was especially touched that it was from his sister, Lucy:

'I have had a parcel from Lucy and a very good one it is too – pork pie and mince pies and lots of other things, so I a not doing so bad, am I? Dear Bertha, remember me when you go to Church during the Christmas week – you know it is my best week in the year, so I ask you most earnestly to think of me and I can assure you I shall think of you. Let me wish you a very happy New Year; I think this letter will be too late to wish you a merry Christmas and let me send my best love to you and the kiddies.'   [23rd *December 1916*]

'May God bless you all and keep you safe and may He bring me back home to you all again.'

[23rd *December 1916*]

The words Jim wrote make it clear that at Christmas he was missing his family more than at any other time since he had been in France – it was traditionally an occasion for children and togetherness and nothing could make up for their being so far apart.

On Christmas Eve, Jim had the opportunity to write a long letter home, one that is entirely given over to thoughts of home, of family and of friends:

'Dear Bertha, I now take the pleasure on this Christmas Eve to write you a few lines. It is the first Christmas that I have been away from you since we first went together. I hope, please God, it will be the last. [Ironically, it was]. I know your prayers at this Christmas time will be for me and my children's will be too. May

Happier times – Jim and Bertha.

God bless you all and may you have a happy Christmas – I know it won't be like the old Christmases as we have always had but I ask you to cheer up and make the best of it. Give my best wishes to Sid, Fred, Jim and all your sisters and brothers and to your mother. I wish I was going to spend my Christmas with you all and to be at the old fireside along with the old boys, singing carols and having one of Butlers' best[1]. Tell them I have missed you all. Keep smiling through it all. I hope, please God, it will soon end.'

[24th *December*]

This heartfelt description gives a brief insight into the traditional family Christmas and if Jim could not be there in person he could certainly be there in mind. His list of people, to thank and to be remembered to, continued:

'I have had a Christmas card from Emmie – I have sent her a field card and I will get her one of those pretty

---

[1] A good Midland brew!

cards. I haven't written to Mr. Wood yet but perhaps after Christmas I will have a chance.' [24th *December*]

The mention of Emmie was repeated from the previous letter:

'I have just had a letter from Emmie and a Christmas card – will you thank her for me? Tell her I haven't got the time to answer her but I wish to be remembered to all at the works and let me wish them a prosperous New Year. I hope, please God, it will be a much better one than this passing one.' [23rd *December*]

Jim's friends at St. Patrick's Church back in Walsall had kindly sent him a Christmas parcel but it had presented Jim with a bit of a dilemma:

'I don't know what to do with the shirt [khaki shirt and socks in a Christmas parcel from the Church] – it is a shame to wear it out here, it will get crummy (lousy). I will see one of the officers and ask him if I can send it home. The socks I can wear here – I can always do with them.' [24th *December*]

The only reference that he made to life in France came towards the end of the letter when he explained what was happening in the battalion rest area over the festive period:

'We are going to have a little bit of enjoyment this Christmas. We are away from the trenches, as I think I have already told you. We are having a rest and we are going to have a feed; at night, we are having a concert and your humble servant is down for singing, so you can see we are not dead yet.' [24th *December*]

Not exactly what Jim was used to back home but it was most assuredly better than being in the trenches as were many poor lads that Christmas. In his usual positive manner, Jim signed off his letter:

'Cheer up, old girl, and keep on smiling for who knows, this war may come to an end very shortly and God grant that I may be spared to come home to you all once again. Please remember me to **all** I know this Christmas time. God bless you and our little'uns and keep you safe till I return again.' [24th *December*]

25th December, Christmas Day, was something the Tommies were most definitely not accustomed to – a day off! Next day the training routine was resumed but

Jim's Christmas card to Lucy.

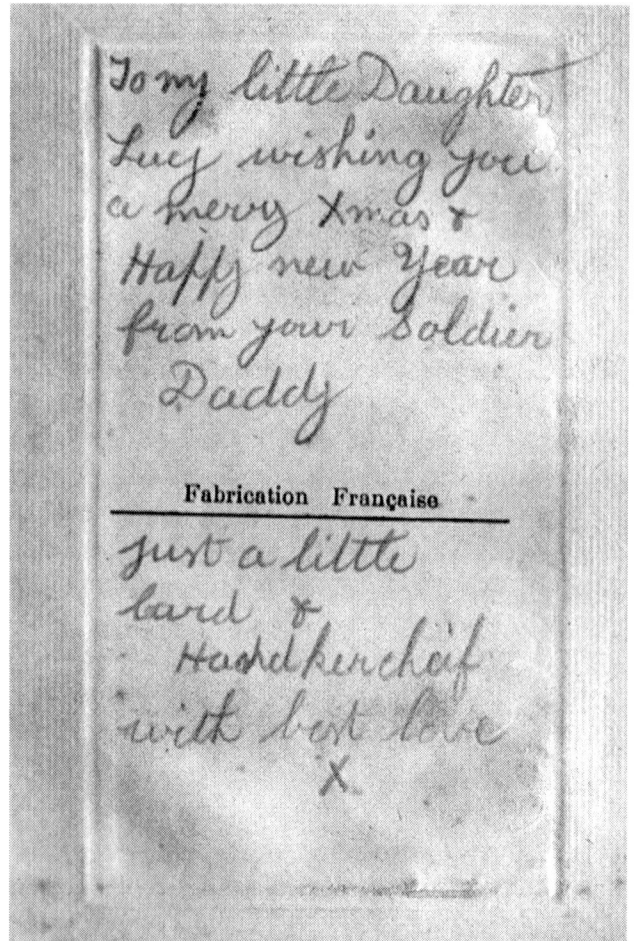

Jim still had plenty of time to write home with news of Christmas in Ambrines:

'I am glad to tell you that we have had, under the conditions in which we are placed, a decent time this Christmas. We had three good feeds on Christmas Day and we also had some Christmas pudding and we finished up at night with a concert and altogether we had a good time.' [28th *December*]

Jim was certainly not forgotten that Christmas as he pointed out:

'Dear Bertha, I have just had a New Year card from S B Jagger [his old employer] – it's a very nice one too and he tells me he sent me a parcel a week before this card was posted. I haven't received it yet nor the one Mrs. Hickson has sent me. Let me wish you all a happy and prosperous New Year.'   [28th *December*]

While the training continued so Jim's letters flowed thick and fast, as did the letters and most of the parcels out to France:

'I have received a parcel from Mr. Jagger and very good one too. It had some Christmas pudding in, some fags, a tin of peaches and a lot of other things. I have written to him to thank him for it.'   [1st *January 1917*]

'Dear Bertha, did you get the Christmas card I sent you (below) because it was a very nice one. I received yours safe, also the one from the kiddies. Have you sent a parcel lately? If you have, I haven't had it.'   [1st *January*]

'If you see the old folks you can tell them I am well and strong and so is Johnny Walker[2] and tell them all I wish them a happy and prosperous New Year.'
[1st *January*]

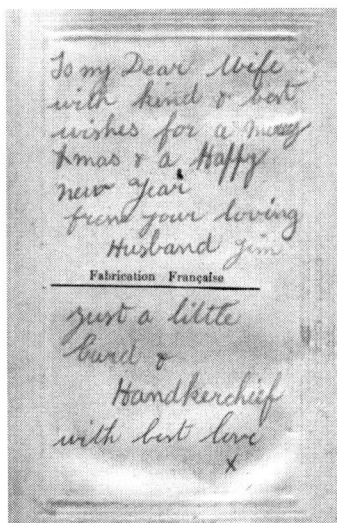

Jim's 1916 Christmas card to Bertha.

At long last, though better late than never, Bertha's letter arrived at Ambrines:

'I have received your Christmas letter, as you call it – I can see you have had a jolly time. I dare say it cost you a little bit of money to rig them out (Lizzie and Lucy) this Christmas, things being so dear[3]. I can see by your letter you have got them almost everything new. You can tell them their daddy says that Santa Claus must have been very kind to bring them a big tree like that and place it there under their daddy's photo. But you were very silly not to stay at Fred's (next door) for the Christmas time, you would have been alright.'
[4th *January*]

Occasionally, Jim tended to repeat the things that he had said in previous letters but there is little surprising in this:

'We did have a decent time (at Christmas) – it was far better than being in the trenches…we had some good feeds…and a concert at night and I had to sing but I think my voice gets too weak for singing now but anyway I did my best.'   [8th *January*]

There was, however, one matter that was concerning Jim quite a lot:

'I am waiting for those mince pies and the cake to come.'
[8th *January*]

The British Tommy always managed to get his priorities right!

Jim and 7th Suffolk had been remarkably fortunate in that their period of rest and training coincided with Christmas and the New Year. Many lads were enduring Christmas in the mud and cold of the trenches where there was most certainly no repetition of the unofficial Christmas truce that had so infuriated the British High Command in December 1914. The training went ahead apace; what the lads of 7th Suffolk did not know was that the time spent out of the trenches would be paid back in lives and blood during the spring offensive that has come to be known to history as the Battle of Arras.

Going back into the line - '…sometimes you get so far in the rear, marching in, you are as good as lost when you come to a spot where different trenches branch off.'

[2] This is probably a platoon nickname for Alf Walker, a word play on the popular brand of Scotch Whisky.
[3] A clear reference to the rise in prices that was making it so difficult for Bertha to make ends meet.

CHAPTER FIVE

'...it's going to be hell this spring and there are a lot yet to go under...'

LETTER 21

[Thursday 28 December 1916.
Written to Bertha and the girls.]

Boxing Day notwithstanding, the battalion went straight back into serious training at Ambrines after the Christmas festivities but Jim had nothing to say in his letter about the new routine; this may have been in respect of censorship but more likely the mental relaxation that came with increased distance from the front line. His main concern was for the health of his family who had not been too well:

'Just a few lines in answer to your kind and welcome letter and New Year card which I received today (Wednesday) 27th and one which I shall keep along with all the others. I am sorry to hear that you haven't had the cards and handkerchiefs.

'I am very pleased to hear that my little'uns are better and you too. I am in the pink again. My feet have been bad but they are much better now. Please let me know about my little Lucy and Lizzie, if they are better and our Nell too [Nell had been in hospital before Christmas].'

The postal service had apparently produced something of a backlog from the Christmas period:

'Did you ask Jim Powell to thank those at Broadhursts for the fags they sent me and tell him I will try to write them a letter soon.'

'Dear Bertha, I have just had a New Year card from S. B. Jagger – it's a very nice one too and he tells me he sent me a parcel a week before this card was posted. I haven't received it yet nor the one Mrs. Hickson has sent me.'

Jim signed off with his customary:

'God be with you all till we meet again.'

FIELD SERVICE POSTCARD 22

[Sunday 31 December 1916.
Written to Bertha and the girls.]

On this occasion, Jim chose to send a field service postcard rather than write a letter. It is probable that 'D' Company or even the whole battalion was away from camp on manoeuvres as part of their training schedule for the expected spring offensive. As usual, he was allowed to communicate only the bare minimum of information:

'I am quite well.
'Letter follows at first opportunity.'

LETTER 23

[Monday 1st January 1917.
Written to Bertha and the girls.]

New Year's Day 1917. It may seem strange to note that Jim sent a field postcard the day before a proper letter but it is necessary to appreciate, eighty years on, that the lower ranks were rarely informed of where they were going that day, let alone the possibility of where they would be during the following week or so. As a result, a man wrote home, in whatever form, whenever the opportunity arose and in Jim's case this resulted in a run of six

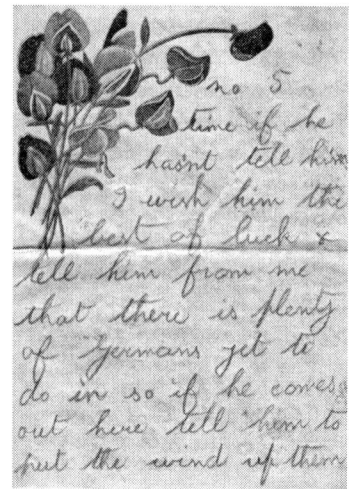

Part of Jim's New Year letter to Bertha.

letters in the space of twelve days. Most of this short letter related to Christmas parcels and letters and is dealt with in the previous chapter:

'Have you sent a parcel lately? If you have, I haven't had it.'

'If you see the old folks you can tell them I am well and strong and so is Johnny Walker and tell them all I wish them a happy and prosperous New Year.'

'God bless you and the children and keep you well and safe till I come home again.'

LETTER 24

[Thursday 4 January 1917.
Written to Bertha and the girls.]

Once again, this letter is largely concerned with the aftermath of the Christmas period and as such is largely covered in the previous chapter. However, there was one bone of contention – Bertha had taken it into her head that Jim was in hospital, perhaps as a result of Jim mentioning in an earlier letter that he had visited the doctor and thought he was developing a bad case of trench foot:

'I am not in hospital as you thought and my feet are much better now but I am sorry to tell you I am not as well as I should like to be. I think I shall be right again in a day or two – it's a nasty cold I have on me, so there is no need to worry.'

Bouts of trench foot were a common and almost inevitable side effect of serving in the front line, as were colds that sometimes developed into the dreaded pneumonia. If one reflects upon the conditions that the men endured, then it is not so much surprising that so many men fell ill but surprising that it was so few.

Tucked away at the end of his letter, Jim refers to some cards (similar to the one shown below) that he had sent home. These were most likely the embroidered cards that were so popular among the Tommies, so

Silk-embroidered card: 'Glory'.

much so that they were not always readily available, thus Jim had been pleased to obtain a few to send home. He also mentions writing to his mother, Martha. It is a pity that only one of his letters to her (Letter 48 on page 65) remains as they would have afforded an insight into another aspect of Jim's life:

'I am glad to know you got those cards alright – I hope you like them. Tell my mother I will write her soon. God bless you all.'

LETTER 25

[Friday 5 January 1917. Written to Bertha and the girls.]

7th Suffolk's training could not have been too time-consuming during the first week of the New Year as Jim settled down just a day later to write yet another missive:

'...I am in the best, now. In my last letter I told you I was not so well as I should like to be but I feel a treat now, so cheer up, old girl, don't be downhearted. I don't know where you got that about me being in the hospital but I am not. You don't go with little things like that.

'Is my little Lucy getting better, you didn't say so in your last letter. I hope you are not keeping anything back from me; please tell me in your next letter then I can rest well.'

One of Jim's greatest fears was that he would not know all that was happening to his little girls and the thought of one or both of them being ill, far beyond his capacity to do anything to help them, must have wrenched at his mind. With no news of the trenches to fill his pages, Jim turned his attention to what was happening, '...*in the old town*'. From this part of the letter it is possible to glean that Bertha worked in a shop in Walsall in order to try to make ends meet:

'How are you getting on in Walsall now, I mean with the food? I suppose by now it's a high price so let me ask you not to send me more than you can afford. I know you have enough to do to look after yourself and the kiddies. How is the trade in the town now? Are they busy and how are your shop girls and old Jack Jurdy (the spelling of this name is never clear in any of Jim's letters) – remember me to him and please remember me to all my old shop mates and all the girls. I have written to Mr. Jagger to thank him for his parcel.'

At this point Jim's thoughts turned to young Sid Powell, nineteen year-old son of his friends and relatives Sid and Maria Powell, who was waiting to be called into the army. Jim was only too aware of what awaited the lad and he consequently tried to make light of it:

'Has young Sid gone up yet? It's getting near his time. If he hasn't, tell him I wish him the best of luck and tell him from me there are plenty of Germans yet to do in, so if he comes out here tell him to put the wind up them and look cheerful about it. But I hope he will never have to come out here. Let us hope, please God, it will all be over before he is ready. Let me know about Tom Spencer, whether he has gone out.'

Tom Spencer was Jim's brother-in-law by virtue of being married to Jim's sister Rosetta (known as Rose) and was already in the army but at that time he was training in England and was evidently liable to be drafted abroad at any moment. Nothing more is known of his army service but Tom would survive the war.

Jim signed off with his usual:

'God bless you all and may He look down upon us all and grant us peace.'

LETTER 26

[Monday 8 January 1917. Written to Bertha and the girls.]

Jim's 'Little'uns – Lizzie and Lucy.

This letter was undoubtedly preceded by the arrival of a letter from home bearing mixed news of the family's health:

'I am glad my little Lucy is getting better and I hope they will make a cure of her and you. Dear Bertha, you must not worry so much – you must be brave and bear it. You can't expect to be well if you are going to keep on the worry all the time. Is my little Lizzie alright? I often think of her, how her little eyes used to fill with tears when we spoke of her Uncle Fred and I know they do when you speak of me. I pray God will soon end it all and bring me back to you and the little'uns (below left) once more.

'Tell the children… their Daddy says they must be good little girls and then God will bring me back to them again.

'I am very sorry to hear of Mother and Dad being so bad but I trust by the time you get this letter they will be a good deal better.'

One can but imagine the turmoil that such news must have engendered and Jim probably felt that the only way forward was, as usual, to put on a brave face.

Jim took the opportunity to explain to Bertha the custom in the trenches of sharing the good things that were sent out from Blighty[1]:

'About the parcels – I do share them but they don't all do that but I will keep to myself what you asked me to.'

Though some things never seemed to arrive when expected:

'I am waiting for those mince pies and the cake to come.'

Apparently a letter had arrived from Sid and Maria Powell in which Sid talked about how they would celebrate Jim's return from the front line:

'You can tell Sid that if God spares me to come home we will have the time he speaks of. Tell him all he can do is pray for me to come back safe.

'God be with us till we meet again. PS: remember me to all I know.'

LETTER 27

[Saturday 13 January 1917.
Written to Bertha and the girls.]

At almost the same time as Sid and Maria's letter arrived, so did one from their son, young Sid, who had evidently decided to volunteer for army service before he was sent for:

'I had a letter from young Sid a few days ago and he tells me he's going up this month. Silly, young fool, why doesn't he wait till it's his time to go up – he will have

---

[1] The soldiers' name for Britain or home.

enough of it, I can tell you but I suppose he wants to get into the Flying Corps, that's the reason he wants to go. Tell him I wish him the best of luck and tell him to look sharp and learn to fly and come over here to see if he can find me and I'll have a fly with him. Tell him to learn how to fetch the German machines down, lots of them. If ever we see theirs and ours having a tussle in the air it's a hundred to one that Fritz has got to come to the ground and sometimes in a devil of a hurry – you can always have your little bet on our chap. Fritz is a clever fellow, I'll admit, but he's not clever enough for our lads in the air, that's one thing we are on top with. So give Siddy that tip – he's going on the winning side in that respect.'

It is possible that young Sid thought that by volunteering he would stand a better chance of fulfilling his aim of joining the Royal Flying Corps[2]. However, to enter the RFC a man had to initially join an army regiment and then apply to become a flier from there. Unfortunately, Jim was wrong in his assessment of young Sid joining the '...*winning side*' in the air. German pilots tended to be better trained and more experienced, while their aircraft were without doubt superior; young British pilots were being pitched into the front line with fewer than twenty hours solo time in the air and their life expectancy in combat was not much longer than that. As for their machines, the Germans were now equipped with the new Albatross D.III, while the British aircraft, such as the FE2b, were outgunned and outperformed. The ensuing few months of spring 1917 would witness slaughter in the skies above Arras.

Time away from the wet and cold of the trenches had afforded Jim's painful feet an opportunity to recover, though he was aware that the respite was but temporary:

'I feel better now than I have done for a long time. It may be the rest that is doing me good but it will soon be over now and then away we go again to the trenches for God knows how long – in my opinion, for a long time yet, for I can't see how this war is going to come to a finish yet awhile.'

Contact with home always managed to make Jim feel a good deal better. Besides, it enabled him to put in his order for the next parcel:

'Thank and kiss my little Lizzie for her letter to her Daddy – I wish I could do it myself.

'You will think I am always on the beg but forgive me, won't you? Will you please send me some envelopes – I want them badly and I can't get them out here; (also) some razor blades and handkerchiefs – I have only got one in the world and if I happen to lose that I'm done.'

One of 'those photos' - Bertha, Lizzie, Jim and Lucy with Nell Webster.

'Dear Bertha, you never told me how those photos turned out, you know, those that I had taken at the same time as we had them taken together (see the example above). I should like to have seen them. I'll bet you've got one, you old fox.'

Jim signed off by sending his regards to his close friends and family:

'Give my best wishes to Fred and Teresa, Sid and Maria, your mother and to Harry (Webster, see photo on page 50) and to all of them – I can't mention all their names as there's too many. Wish them a happy and prosperous New Year. And let me ask you, Dear Bertha and the little'uns, to accept the same and my very best love.'

'God bless you all and keep you safe and may He, in His mercy, bring me back to you and the children once again.'

LETTER 28
[Monday 15 January 1917.
Written to Bertha and the girls.]

On 14th January, the day before this letter was written, 12th 'Eastern' Division received orders to take over duties in the sector east of Arras, the line from Faubourg

[2] For the first three and a half years of the war pilots flew either with the RFC or with the Royal Naval Air Service (RNAS); on 1st April 1918 the two branches joined to form the Royal Air Force.

St. Sauveur to the River Scarpe. However, Jim and his mates of 7th Suffolk were lucky as only one brigade (comprising four battalions) was required in the trenches and it was 37th Brigade that was selected for duty while Jim's 35th Brigade (7th Suffolk, 7th Norfolk, 9th Essex and 5th Royal Berkshire) and 36th Brigade remained in their respective training areas.

Jim with brother-in-law, Harry Webster.

As ever, the army postal service had recently been playing its usual tricks:

'...I write in answer to your kind and welcome letter that I received today......I have written to my mother....the letters must get delayed or lost.

'I asked you to send me some blades but....don't send any more till I ask you. You can send the fags on if you like but not the tobacco. I wrote to Mr. Wood yesterday but ....forgot to thank him for the fags. You say Maria is writing me and will make me smile – I hope she will succeed. I should also like to know what your surprise is – if it is anything to wear, Bertha, don't send it as I have plenty of changes so you need not worry about that. I had your registered letters with the money in before Christmas I am glad to hear that Rose (Tom Spencer's wife and Jim's sister) is going on alright – I hope she will keep it up now.'

By now it seemed that young Sid Powell had been called away to basic training and Jim accepted the reality in the knowledge of what the lad had let himself in for:

'I am sorry that young Sid has gone but tell him to keep a good heart and that I wish him the best of luck.'

Alf Walker was still in the same platoon as Jim and he was, as ever, in good spirits:

'Alf Walker is alright and wishes to be remembered to you – he's just had a parcel come so we are right again for a bit now.'

Jim signed off as usual:

'God bless you and my little'uns.'

LETTER 29
[Thursday 25 January 1917.
Written to Bertha and the girls.]

This letter was written while the battalion was still in training at Ambrines and the following day, 26th January, 7th Suffolk and the entire 35th Brigade was to be inspected by Lieutenant-Colonel F.E. Walter, General Officer Commanding 35th Brigade.

Jim had evidently benefited from the extended period out of the line:

'I am much better now than I have been.'

However, his improved health was more than counterbalanced by the frustrations of the army postal service:

'Dear Bertha, I haven't received your parcel yet and...I think it's gone west. I am sorry because I think it must

Alf 'Johnny' Walker wearing South Staffords' cap badge.

have cost you a lot of money – it must be a big loss to you. I have just received a letter from my mother with some fags in it and it was broken open. I can't say how many she put in but there were two packets in when I got it and half of them were broken. There were only four good ones. Johnny (Alf) Walker (pictured left) says he is sorry the parcel hasn't come because he can't have his cake. He still has the doll you put in the last one and he says he's coming back to Walsall to bring it back to you, (though) when I can't say.'

From Jim's next comments it becomes clear that young Sid had worked as an iron-caster with his father prior to call up. Yet there was a sting in the tail of the paragraph:

'I haven't had Maria's letter yet. I suppose by now young Sid has gone. I daresay our Sid has missed him. Who has he got working with him now? How are Fred and Teresa going on – tell Fred to save a drop of petrol for me because I shall want a good ride (in his motor car) when I come home. Will you please ask Jim if they received that letter I sent to Broadhursts. Dear Bertha, did you hear of young George Jones getting done in? I knew him well, you know. We were together a lot at Scotton – I feel very sorry for his Mother.'

Even though the 'Pals' idea had been officially discontinued after the horrific effects on communities when the casualty lists of 1st July on the Somme reached home, many lads still signed up together from the same locality, went through training together and faced the rigours of trench life together. So, when a local man was killed, the ripple often ran deep with word spreading on the grapevine and reaching home through letters such as Jim's. George Jones had been through much of his basic training at Scotton in the South Staffordshire Reserve with Jim but, unlike his friend, had remained with the regiment although he was transferred to 7th Battalion. This battalion had previously seen service from August to September 1915 on the dreaded Gallipoli Peninsula, had served in the Suez Canal Zone until June 1916 and had then been returned to France for duty on the Somme. When twenty year-old George Jones had reached 7th South Staffordshire, in mid-September, they were about to embark upon two battles on the Somme that were to cost the battalion twenty-four dead and countless more wounded.

George Jones's headstone, at Contay British Cemetery, Somme, France.

The battalion was withdrawn from the line on 1st October but over the ensuing two months saw frequent line-holding service on the Somme, losing another sixty-three men killed, among them George Jones from the effects of poison gas. George was gassed on Wednesday, 29th November and was quickly moved down the line towards Amiens where he was treated in either Number 9 or Number 49 Casualty Clearing Station at Contay. Sadly, George Jones never recovered and died within hours that same day; he is buried in plot VII. A. 33 of Contay British Cemetery on the Somme (shown above). George had been born and bred in Walsall and lived with his mother at 104, Wolverhampton Street; he was a single man and had been employed in the Birmingham Canal Toll Office at West Bromwich. His death must have come as an especially bitter blow to his mother, Ellen, who had already lost her husband, William, prior to her son being called up by the army. War was a hard taskmaster.

Consequently, Jim's signing off was even more heartfelt than usual:

'God bless you all and may God in His mercy grant us peace and bring me back home to you all once again. God be with us till we meet again.'

LETTER 30
[Tuesday 30 January 1917.
Written to Bertha and the girls.]

By the morning of 30th January, the battalion was cleared away and awaiting the order to move off from Ambrines. The village had been their home for more than a month and the troops had rendered even the poor-quality billets reasonably habitable; the men were expecting to be sent back into the line near Arras but yet again they were to be proven wrong.

Jim took advantage of the brief lull in proceedings to quickly run off what was his first letter for six days; yet it was a much longer time since he had received one from his family, though a couple had arrived from friends:

'Dear Bertha, this is the fourth letter I have written to you since I had one from you – I can't understand it, where your letters get to, I'm sure. Don't think I am putting the blame on you, Dear Bertha, I know you have written me – the letters must get lost or delayed.

'I had a letter from Mr. Stanley yesterday and a very nice letter too – you see, they have not forgotten me at the works. I have also had one from Emmie – I haven't had time to reply yet, so please thank her for me and tell her I will write the first chance I get.'

Having been in relatively permanent billets for so long, certain items had come into short supply or were exceedingly expensive:

'Dear Bertha, if you could get one or two candles off Mr. Wood [at S.B. Jagger's shop] I should be very pleased – they cost so much money here – you can't get them for less than 2d each and often you can't get them at all.'

Sitting around waiting for the battalion to move prompted Jim to say more than usual about his good mate Alf:

'I am pleased to tell you that Johnny (Alf) Walker is alright and still going strong. He's here ripping the rag – he's got more to say than any old woman. I can tell you, he's all rattle, like a stone in a can.'

Calling Alf by the name 'Johnny', which almost certainly was his nickname in the platoon, and using the phrase, 'still going strong', have their origins in a popular Scotch Whisky and its principal advertisement that was current at that time – 'Johnny Walker (whisky), still going strong after all these years!'

Jim was also very keen to keep in touch with the people of his parish church, St. Patrick's, in North Walsall:

'How are all the folks at home and my friends at the Church? Please remember me to them all.

'God bless you and the children and may He in His mercy bring me back home to you all once again.'

LETTER 31
[Sunday 4 February 1917.
Written to Bertha and the girls.]

At half-past midday on 30th January the battalion moved off along the narrow roads towards Duisans, ten miles nearer Arras but though they were moving towards the sound of the guns they were not due into their range yet awhile. A brisk march brought the battalion to their billets in Duisans by 5 p.m. and, after a makeshift meal, the men set about the task of organising their quarters. A decent night's sleep later, the lads were wondering what their next orders would be – they were soon told that the battalion was to be employed as a 'labour' battalion for a short time. Their first task, commencing on 31st January, was to help build a new railway between Agnez-lès-Duisans (less than a mile west of the billets) and Acq; as this would constitute about three miles of entirely new track it represented a tough assignment (see map on page 13).

By 4th February, the day this letter was written, Jim and his mates had been working on the railway line for five days and were glad of a brief break on the Sunday:

'I am glad to tell you Johnny Walker is alright – he is still with me and still going strong. How is the weather in old Blighty? It's cold and frosty here – I hope it will soon get a bit warmer.'

The frost that Jim writes about seems to have been most severe and almost certainly made the task of building the railway more arduous, though it had an unexpected side effect on one of his parcels:

'I am very pleased to tell you I have received your parcel that was dated 10th January [three weeks late] – I had given it up so you can guess how surprised I was when it came. I enjoyed very much…. what you spoke of; it was the first thing I found and it was the first I shifted out of sight, you can bet. The bananas and the oranges were frozen and they were like ice itself but all the mince pies and cake and all the rest of the contents were in good condition and they were great, I can tell you.'

Three weeks in transit cannot have helped the condition of the parcel's contents but hungry soldiers are rarely put off by such minor considerations and Jim was obviously feeling good:

'I am at present in the best of health. I am longing to know how you all are, it seems such a while since I heard from you. I have just had a letter from my Mother (but) I haven't read it yet. It was all broken open again – please tell them…. to use a stronger envelope.'

As was so often the case, Jim's main concern was not for his own plight but for that of his friends and family back in Walsall:

'I dare say poor old Sid is feeling it, and by the by, how is young Siddy going on? Where has he gone to? If you can let me know I should be very pleased. Did they receive that letter I sent to the fireside? Will you ask Jim Powell (if) he's alright and MaryAnn (Bertha's sister) and the kiddies too. Remember me to all I know, especially to your people.

'(Tell) the children that their Daddy sends them a big kiss for the chocolate.'

Chocolate was one of Jim's favourite treats and he loved to open a parcel that produced a bar or two. He signed off in his usual manner:

'God bless you all.'

LETTER 32
[Tuesday 6 February 1917.
Written to Bertha and the girls.]

6th February was the battalion's final day of working on the new Duisans to Acq railway and the Battalion War Diary records:

The war-damaged Bishop's Palace in Arras.

'6/2/17. Working Battalion. Working on railway; in the evening left for Arras; arrived Arras 8 p.m. Took over billets used when in Arras before.'

This clearly refers to the billets previously used in Arras (for three companies), in Achicourt (one company) and in Ronville (one company) indicating that the battalion was in the reserve line. The reason for this would become apparent next morning. The roll of the dice was again kind to 7th Suffolk and 35th Brigade for it was to be 36th Brigade that was selected to relieve 37th Brigade in the trenches. 35th Brigade's allotted task would, however, take them into the line but for a different reason.

Ever the resourceful soldier, Jim refused to throw away the frozen fruit and managed to warm it sufficiently to enable him and his mates to polish it off:

'...I have received the parcel with the handkerchiefs and the photo – thanks very much for them. The cake and mince pies (in the other parcel) were very good and also the chocolate but the fruit was frozen. I had to warm it up before I could eat it but I managed it alright, you can bet. The other was great – me and Johnny Walker had that for ourselves.'

The final reference remains a mystery but it was most certainly some 'goodies' that Jim wanted to keep to himself and Alf. The rest of the letter is concerned with sorting out one or two minor problems and demonstrates that people at home were more than willing to lend a helping hand:

'...are you sending the (razor) blade along with the gloves? Let me know what to expect.

'I didn't quite understand you about the money but anyway you can let me know if you should succeed and I will write to Mr. Stanley to thank him for his trouble – I think it's very kind of him to take so much worry and interest on my behalf. May God bless him for it now.'

Jim signed off with his usual short prayer:

'May God bless you and the kiddies and keep you safe and bring me back to you all once again.'

But he couldn't resist the postscript – you can almost see Jim grinning as he writes:

'PS: Johnny Walker is still going strong.'

LETTER 33
*[Saturday 10 February 1917.
Written to Bertha and the girls.]*

Having moved into the old reserve line billets, the men of 7th Suffolk must have believed that their 'holiday' away from the guns had come to an end but that proved to be far from the truth. The ensuing fortnight saw the entire battalion continuing in its role as a labour battalion when it was set the task of improving dugouts in Arras No.1 sector. Digging into the frozen ground was backbreaking work yet conversely, when there was a later thaw, whole sections of trench often caved in as iron-hard ground turned to soft mud:

A British battalion at work in better conditions.

'It has been awfully cold out here for some time now – they say that last month was the coldest we have had since the war began. I hope it will break soon. I am fairly well at present, with the exception of a little bit of a cold and we have all got that, more or less. Poor old Johnny Walker can't talk for he's lost his voice.'

The last sentence was rather ironic, and frustrating for the victim, as Jim had said in an earlier letter:

'....he's (Johnny Walker) got more to say than any old woman.'   [30th January 1917]

It appears that, contrary to an earlier letter, young Sid had still not been called into the army:

'That's a good little joke of our Sid's about coming over in an aeroplane – the kiddies will keep on looking for a long time, God bless them. You tell Sid from me he's far better off where he is – I only wish I was back in old Blighty. I am very glad that young Siddy is still at home. Good luck to him.'

The rest of this letter is concerned with family matters, especially Jim's worries about one of his daughters:

'….I cannot understand about our little Lucy – what is the matter with her? Don't keep anything back from me, please.

'Thanks very much for the handkerchiefs, they are very good ones but the gloves weren't in (the parcel).

'I send my best love to you and the children and tell them their Daddy thanks them for the handkerchiefs.

'Glad to hear your boss has got a tender (for an order) – I hope he will succeed in getting it and you need not worry about Mr. Jagger – I will write him to thank him for his kindness.'

The possibility of Bertha's boss obtaining a tender for work is important as it would have meant extra money for the family on account of the likelihood of overtime. Jim signed off as usual:

'God bless you all and may He in His mercy bring me safely home to you all once again.'

LETTER 34

[Monday 12 February 1917.
Written to Bertha and the girls.]

As in the previous letter, Jim's battalion was still employed on labour duties, digging new dugouts in the front line and support trenches to the east of Arras. The cold weather was beginning to take its toll on Jim's health and he was in dire need of a good pair of gloves:

'I'm sorry to tell you I'm not in the best of health – I can't get rid of my cold and cough. I am coughing and barking all the time.

'What I want most hasn't yet come and that is the gloves. Let me tell you not to worry about sending big parcels – I am satisfied with small ones. I can guess what you are going through in Blighty but keep on

smiling, old girl, like the old song goes – "there's a silver lining, through the dark clouds shining[3]." So don't worry about me – look after yourself and the children.'

Much of this rather short letter relates to matters at home, from serious concerns about fuel supplies to teasing Maria and to worries about his two daughters:

'I'm glad to hear you did what you did about your coal – I've no doubt you want it in this weather. You can tell Maria [Powell] I am still waiting for that letter – it's taking a lot of pen and ink to write it!

'I will write to Martha [Jim's oldest sister] and the others and thank them (for the parcel). I had a letter from Ted [Jim's brother who was in the army] the other day. I can't write to him because I don't have the letter with his address on.

'Tell the children if they don't be good for their Mother and do what they are told to do I shan't come over in that aeroplane.'

Jim signed off with:

'God be with you till we meet again. PS: remember me to all I know.'

LETTER 35

[Thursday 15 February 1917. Written
to Bertha and the girls.]

The wearying trench work continued, so Jim had little chance to shake off his persistent cough and cold. It was little compensation to hear that the freezing weather was hitting England as well:

'…my cold is a little better – I think I shall be myself again in a few days. It's my cough that's troubling me most – if I could get rid of that I should be alright. I've never had a cough last so long on me.

'I was glad to hear you had got a good stock of coal in because I had a letter from Mother the other day and they tell me that the weather has been so cold it's frozen the canals and they cannot get it (coal) through[4]. Our Nell [Jim's youngest sister] wrote and told me that poor old Dad had to walk all the way down to their house

[3] This line comes from a song popular at the time, *'Keep the home fires burning.'*
[4] At that time the principal method of transporting coal substantial distances was by narrow boat – water transport made light of the heavy weights involved, whereas roads were simply not up to the task. However, ice brought even the canals to a standstill.

and beg a bit to carry on with. Poor old Dad, I dare say it's about done him in this winter and my poor old Mother too.'

The letter from Jim's parents, Joe and Martha, was one among several that had arrived in recent days:

'I got your postcard safe and it's a very pretty one too. I forgot to thank you in my last letter for the photo – do you think it's a good one? What I mean is, if you are satisfied with it, then so am I. I'll put it along with the others.'

'The others' referred to here include at least one photograph of Jim's daughters – this will take on greater significance in chapter eight (see letter 71 on pages 77-78). Another parcel had arrived from Bertha, though it did not contain what he most needed – razor blades:

'Dear Bertha, I shan't take any notice of what is on the parcel, so you won't hurt my feelings and I should never think of you getting tired of sending anything I ask for so long as you can afford it. So, please don't worry, old girl, about that. I am going to start begging again now – I want you to please send me some blades (as) I am on my last one.'

It seems that Jim's former employer, Mr. Jagger, was helping Bertha to sort out a problem; it is likely that this '...*little affair*' related to trying to obtain for Bertha an increase in the Separation Allowance that was intended to supplement a soldier's income in respect of dependents. Mr. Jagger's aid was well received as he was used to dealing with bureaucracy:

'Dear Bertha, let me know how you get on with that little affair, you know what I mean, the one Mr. Jagger is looking into for you and please let me know how you get on.'

Jim's final lines ran as follows:

'Ah well, some day, please God, I will be coming back and cheer you all up again.'
'God bless you all and may He in His mercy grant us peace and bring me back again to you all.'

LETTER 36
[Sunday 26 February 1917.
Written to Bertha and the girls.]

Until 21st February, the battalion remained in its labour role in the trenches but on their return from work that day the order was given to strike camp and start out on the road for the village of Montenescourt, seven miles to the west of Arras. The fortnight had not been without danger, losing one man killed in action (Private Fred Pettitt of Wood Ditton in Cambridgeshire) and several wounded. The march took from 5:45 p.m. until the following morning at 9:00 a.m., when the work-weary troops slumped onto beds in their new billets. Sensibly, the men were given the remainder of 22nd February to rest and clean equipment – the army's equivalent of a day off! On 23rd February there commenced a training programme that, even to the untutored eye, carried the promise of a major, set-piece attack. That day, the men were trained in a new form of line-holding known as the 'outpost scheme'; this required fewer men in the front line (and thus reduced vulnerability to enemy artillery activity) and even removed the need for fully dug, connecting trenches. The idea, one that was to be developed over the ensuing months, was for the front to be held initially by 'island' outposts manned by small numbers of troops, while the main body was held in support or even reserve. The downside was that in a major enemy assault the outposts would be expected to fight to the last before being overwhelmed. Not popular among the men!

7th Suffolk Battalion War Diary clearly indicates the developing intensity of the training:

'24th February – Training; company formation in the attack. 25th February – Training; battalion in attack. 26th February - Route march; practice advance and rearguards.'

The training seems to have covered all eventualities of static defence, advance and retreat!

The move to Montenescourt and the training regime had left Jim with little time for the niceties of writing his usual letters:

'Just a line or two to let you know I am still knocking about. I am very sorry I haven't written to you for such a long time (eleven days) but I hope you will forgive me. We have been on the move again and I really have not had the time to write to you before.
'I am well.... but not so strong as I used to be.

'I received your parcel safely, the one posted on 9th February – thanks very much for the contents, I enjoyed them very much. I haven't had the time to write to Martha [his eldest sister] to thank her for her share but I will try. I have just received your registered letter with the gloves in and the blades – thanks very much for the same.'

Contrary to the record of the war diary, Jim intimates in this letter that he has been back in the trenches, though his description of conditions is clear enough:

'I have been, yes Lizzie, and again in a few days. You know what I mean, don't you? It's not so cold as it has been but it's awfully muddy and sloppy. It's hard work for us in heavy weather.'

Unfortunately for Jim the passage of the cold weather was but temporary and was to return with a vengeance before too long. The heavy training schedule, however, was taking its toll of Jim's now fragile strength:

'Dear Bertha, you ask me what I want (but) I can't tell you. You can send me just what you like – I shall always be thankful, no matter what it is. I must come to a close as it's getting late and I want a bit of a rest so let me send my best love to you and the children, from your loving husband, Jim.

'God bless you all and keep you safe.'

LETTER 37
[Thursday 1 March 1917. Written to Bertha and the girls.]

On 27th, 28th February and 1st March, the men had practised the manoeuvre, 'battalion in attack,' and by then they must have been strongly suspecting that a 'big push' was in the pipeline for some time in the spring. What they did not know was when it would come.

The brevity of Jim's letter reflects the weariness that the constant training was causing and, as ever, he was hoping that other loved ones would not have to share his experiences in the trenches:

'I have had a letter from Sid [Powell] and he has asked me to pack up and come home – I wish I could. What a jolly time we would have but I am afraid it will be a long time before I can do that. If you take it from me this war will last a long while yet; we chaps know out

here better than you do in old Blighty. We are in it so we should know.'

'I was glad to hear that (young) Siddy has not gone yet but his time is getting short now, as is Tom's [Spencer]. I hope they won't be wanted but of course we never know. (Old) Sid talks about coming up (the line); poor old Sid, I should like to see him with full pack on – I should laugh! You can tell him from me, it's harder work than (iron) casting. Will you thank Sid for the card, please, it's a very pretty one and tell him I will try to write to him soon. I (still) haven't had Maria's letter yet.'

The postal service seems to have been serving Jim well at that time:

'I had the parcel safe and enjoyed the contents very much.'

'Dear Bertha, I have received the letter with the blades in; thanks very much for them, also the gloves but that sort ain't much good out here – they soon wear out but still I am still very thankful for them.'

He signed off with an apology and a brief prayer:

'PS: forgive the writing – it's the only bit of lead I have.'
'God bless you all and keep you safe and bring me back to you all again.'

LETTER 38
[Monday 5 March 1917. Written to Bertha and the girls.]

The Battalion War Diary entry for 2nd March is brief but clear:

'Aeroplane scheme; weather rather hazy. Moved to Arras; relieved 7/Royal Sussex; HQ in Rue Gambetta.'

During the day the battalion in training had practised a scheme that enabled infantry on the ground to communicate with the Royal Flying Corps aircraft above the trenches; such contact would, in theory, allow better direction of artillery fire and would facilitate the more rapid sending to higher command any news of the progress of an attack. In reality, the smoke of battle and low cloud often rendered the scheme unworkable. During the late afternoon, 35th Brigade finally replaced 36th Brigade in the trenches and 7th Suffolk relieved 7th Royal Sussex in the usual reserve lines in Arras itself.

Damaged Ursulines Convent, Rue Gambetta, Arras.

Battalion Headquarters were located in Rue Gambetta, close to the Ursuline Convent with its tall tower, a regular target for enemy artillery. Unusually, the battalion spent six rather than four days in reserve and they were worked abnormally hard at night, repairing dugouts and digging a new trench. The weather remained indifferent, though Jim felt:

'....much better than I have been. I shall be very glad when the weather gets better – I think I shall be alright then.'

A much more important matter was on Jim's mind:

'Dear Bertha, you will find in this letter a postcard below and right) enclosed for my little Lucy's (sixth) birthday [on 25th March] – I may have sent it a little too early but you must not let her see it if you can help it. Then you can give it to her or push it under the door on her birthday and then she will get it herself.'

Letters and parcels had been arriving regularly, for which Jim was duly grateful:

'Thank Sid for his letter – I have sent him a field card.
   'I had the parcel safe, also the registered letter with the gloves and blades in – forgive the crossing out but I'm a duffer at writing letters! Thanks very much for all you have sent me; I also received that registered letter from Arthur Dix [later to marry Phoebe Boddice, Jim's niece] with the fags and money in – if you remember, I

Jim's card for Lucy's sixth birthday.

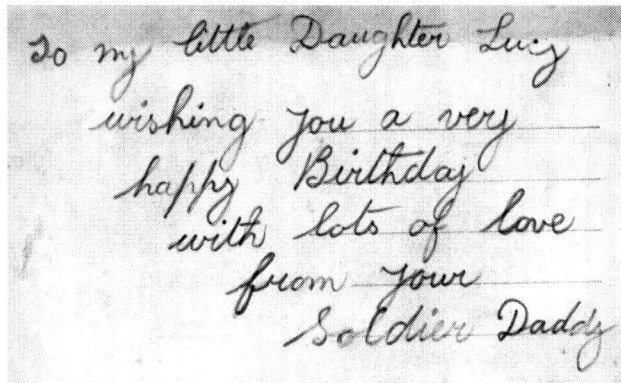

Jim's birthday message for Lucy.

asked you to thank him for me because I cannot write to all. Will you ask Mr. Wood if he can get me a swivel hook to fasten on my belt for my clasp knife. I have lost the one that I had – if he can get one I shall be very glad. He will know what I mean.'

Freddie Wood had worked with Jim at Jagger's and they had evidently developed a close friendship. The request for a swivel hook was important as the clasp knife was something that Jim used frequently in the line. He signed off as usual:

'God be with you till we meet again. Pray for me'

LETTER 39
[Tuesday 6 March 1917. Written to Bertha and the girls.]

The following day Jim found time to write another letter as the deteriorating weather probably curtailed work that night:

'We are still having cold weather here – it's snowing while I am writing this letter but it's not so bad as it has been.
   'Bertha, old girl, you ask me to take care of myself; I am trying to do my best to come back safe and sound. God knows best whether I shall do or not; if it is His will that I go under, my girl, I shall have to go and if it is His will that I come home safe and well, I shall come. But if you believe me, Dear Bertha, it's going to be hell this spring and there are a lot (of men) yet to go under....They mean to decide it this spring, one way or the other, so let me ask you, Bertha, to pray for me more than ever and to keep on smiling for, who knows, I may come home sooner than we think – God grant it be so.'

By now, the grapevine was hot with rumours of a major spring offensive and Jim knew that, after all the training, 7th Suffolk was likely to be in the thick of it. His comment, '*...may come home sooner than we think...*' could have two interpretations – either it might refer to an (unlikely) breakthrough and ending the war or (more realistically) Jim might, '*cop a Blighty one[5]*' and be shipped home.

Of more immediate concern to Jim were his shaving tackle and the letters he had sent to sister Lucy:

'I found the two blades (inside your letter). I will keep all the old ones I have now and send them on to you – I have been throwing them away because I could not get them touched up for me.

'I have had Lucy's [Jim's sister] two parcels and wrote back each time, thanking her for them. The letters must have got lost if she has not heard from me. I never missed a week without writing one (letter to you) at least. I was glad my Mother liked her postcard but you don't say how you liked yours. If you have not had it, let me know. I had a lovely letter from Sid a few days ago but I have not had time to reply yet. When is Maria going to send hers? I should think that the time she's been writing it will reach from London to Berlin! Remember me to Sid and Maria and the kiddies, (also) to Jim and MaryAnn [one of Bertha's sisters]. I have got the photo of her and the baby (see page 33). Remember me to Fred and Teresa, your mother, Nell, Sophia, Lizzie, Harry, Fred and to all I know.

'Remember me to all I know and don't forget my shop-mates.

Jim signed off in almost heartrending fashion:

'Give my best love and kisses to my little Lizzie and Lucy. Teach them, my girl, to pray for their Daddy – I should love to see them and you too, once again.'

'God bless you all and keep you safe and bring me back to you again.'

LETTER 40

[Thursday 8 March 1917. Written to Bertha and the girls.]

Still in the reserve lines, Jim managed to write yet again to Bertha, this time including matters that he had forgotten to mention two days previously:

'The kiddies, God bless them....must be growing quite fast – I shall hardly know them if God spares me to come home again.'

'Dear Bertha, you were vexed, I know, when you knew you had failed by not getting what you wanted but don't grieve over it, old girl, you tried your best and lost. It was very kind of Mr. Jagger to make the running for you – I will write to him to thank him for his trouble. I dare say he wishes I were back with him. So do I, as we always got on well together – the others often wondered how it was.'

'Don't forget to ask Mr. Wood for that swivel hook for my belt.'

It thus appears that Bertha had not been successful in her efforts to obtain an increase in her Separation Allowance, although Mr. Jagger had done his best to secure it. Sid and Maria had yet again sent to Jim (seemingly enclosing a local paper) and this naturally brought to Jim's mind young Sid's situation:

'Let me ask you to thank Sid and Maria for their gift – God bless them and theirs for it. Has Siddy gone yet? I see in the Walsall paper that some have gone so I suppose he is amongst them. Tell him to buck up for we mean to beat the Germans this time around.'

Jim signed off as usual:

'God bless you all and keep you safe and well and bring me back home to you all once again.

'PS: Dear Bertha, you will find enclosed in this letter a picture postcard. I hope you will like it.'

LETTER 41

[Wednesday 14 March 1917.
Written to Bertha and the girls.]

The day after Jim's previous letter, the Battalion War Diary recorded:

'Relieved 7/Royal Berkshire in I2 sub-sector [in front of Arras]. 'A' and 'B' companies in front line, 'C' and 'D' companies in reserve.'

So for the moment, Jim's luck held as his company was for the time being kept in either support or reserve, avoiding what the war diary indicated as having been quite a lively period in the front line:

'10th March - enemy fairly active with Trench Mortars on front line. Our artillery were wire-cutting in

[5] A 'Blighty one' was a wound that was serious enough to cause a man to be treated back in England ('Old Blighty') but not bad enough to cripple him.

morning. 11th March - enemy active; whole sector shelled heavily at about 3:30 a.m., lasting till 4:50 a.m. Trench Mortars used. 12th March - enemy active with Trench Mortars on sector at various times; also shelled line at 2:30 p.m., 5:15 p.m., 10:45 p.m. Very wet and muddy in trenches. 13th March - fairly quiet; trenches on left bombarded. 14th March - in the morning, about 4:00 a.m., an enemy patrol came up to our wire and was fired on; 3 prisoners captured unwounded and one wounded but died later. Otherwise, quiet during day. Usual artillery at night, 5-6:00 p.m.'

From a personal point of view, Jim commented:

'I am much better now than I have been for a long time.'

Yet there must have been a touch of unspoken envy on hearing his brother Ted (pictured below) had obtained another short spell of leave:

Ted Elwell in uniform.

'I was glad to hear that Ted is going on alright and having another leave. You say he's been to see you – I am pleased he's not forgotten you.'

Particularly so because it was soon to be little Lucy's birthday:

'You will by now have received the postcard I sent for Lucy's birthday – I cannot send anything else but she will think a little of that, I know, when she knows it has come from her Dad. I shall get one for Lizzie and send it on – if I don't she will make a fuss over it, I know.'

Jim had been told more than two weeks previously that Bertha was intending to post one of her home-made cakes to him; its non-arrival was most frustrating for men starved of treats:

'Dear Bertha, I have not yet had the parcel you posted on February 28th – I hope it will be coming along soon for I can do with a little bit of your cake. It's been such a long while since I had some of yours, so you see I am longing to get a bite. Will you please thank my Mum and Dad for that money they gave to you.'

Jim signed off with his usual short prayer:

'God bless you all. May He in His mercy bring me back to you all once again.'
'PS: I hope you have received the postcard I sent you and Lucy. Oh, and thank our Nelly too for the money she gave you.'

LETTER 42
[Monday 19 March 1917. Written to Bertha and the girls.]

The battalion had just spent a much longer time than usual in the trenches, eight full days, and things had become livelier as the tour progressed. The Battalion War Diary paints a clear picture:

'15th March - very quiet, early morning. About 5:10 a.m., a hostile raiding party came over, heavy barrage of 77mm shells on right by India Lane[6] [7th Suffolk was on the extreme right flank of 12th Division, with 3rd Division to its right]; they got into our trench on the extreme right and caught one Lewis gunner post. The Battalion of 8/East Yorkshire on left [of 3rd Division] badly handled[7], reached their support line and bombed dugouts. Raiders returned; our casualties, 5 killed, 13 wounded and 3 missing; most casualties due to barrage. 16th March - quiet day, relieved by 9/Essex and went to billets under (Arras) Cathedral.'

On the night of 16th March the battalion moved into support and, as usual, was told off for night-time working parties for the duration. A number of German shells had hit Rue Pasteur near Battalion Headquarters on 17th but the men had been in the caves under the cathedral and, while those billets were perpetually damp, they were certainly shellproof. To gain a modicum of revenge on behalf of 35th Brigade for the damaging German raid on 15th March, the 5th Royal Berkshire carried out a successful trench raid on enemy lines on 17th and raised everyone's spirits. However, although Jim was personally in good nick, the German raid had come as a hard blow:

'...(I am) better than I have been for a long time.'
'I am sorry to tell you that two of our chaps that came out with me have got hit (in the German raid on 15th March). One of them is wounded and (has had) one leg or both off. He is on the photo (of the South

---

[6] A trench name.
[7] Criticism of the handling of battalions, especially of another division, on a flank (where a battalion was very vulnerable), was quite common in war diaries.

Staffordshire platoon at Scotton Camp) and he is a Walsall chap too – Townrow is his name; you know him, I think. The other chap is on the photo too – they cannot say where he is [one of the three men missing in action].'

The lad that Jim referred to, Frank Townrow, was born in Chesterfield, Derbyshire in 1876 or 1877 (and was thus two years older than Jim) but he had moved to Walsall (whether with his parents, for work or as a result of getting married is unknown) and was living at 72, Whitehouse Street. Married to Ellen and father of five children, Frank was employed as a stock-taker at the Birmingham branch of Butler's (of Wolverhampton) Springfield Brewery. He enlisted in Birmingham in June 1916 in the South Staffordshire at the same time and probably in the same place as Jim Elwell (his regimental number, 2599, was eight different from Jim's 2607). Like Jim, Frank Townrow went out to France to join 1/6th South Staffordshire on 16th September 1916 and was almost immediately transferred to 7th Suffolk (where he became 40637, Private Frank Townrow) with the draft that preceded Jim's (number 40659 in 7th Suffolk). Frank died on Tuesday, 15th March 1917, aged 39, of wounds sustained in the German dawn trench raid. As Jim said, Frank Townrow lost one or both legs in the attack and though severely wounded, he was quickly moved eight miles down the line to the

Frank Townrow's headstone, Habarcq, France.

operating centre at Habarcq. Sadly, the efforts were in vain and Frank is buried in plot V. L. 4 of Habarcq Communal Cemetery Extension, Pas de Calais, France (shown above). Three of Frank Townrow's brothers served their country, Ernest and Roland in the army and William in the Royal Flying Corps – it appears that they all survived the war. The other local man referred to in Jim's letter remains unidentified and his fate thus unknown.

There had apparently been a good deal of speculation in the English press about a spring offensive and Bertha seems to have mentioned it in her previous letter. Jim, for obvious reasons, could not comment directly but he did write:

'Don't you take any notice of any rumours, just keep on smiling and hoping for the best but I can tell you this – it's going to be hot and the Germans will find it's hotter than hell.'

It also appears that Sid Powell had done Jim or Bertha a big favour and Jim was most grateful:

'Give my kind regards and best thanks to poor old Sid – if God spares me to come home again I will try any way to pay him back for his kindness. Tell him he cannot do too much for a good brother-in-law [this confirms that Sid's wife Maria was Bertha's sister] – I will punch the sand for him, make his odd side or pour his heats for him and tell him to keep on wondering (where I am). The only conclusion he will come to is somewhere in France.'

The references to '…*punching sand*' and the like relate to iron-casting, Sid Powell's trade.

Jim had again sent home a couple of the silk postcards that were so popular among the soldiers serving in Belgium and France; surprisingly, Jim says he didn't need any money, which was unusual:

'I have sent on two more postcards, one each for the kiddies. You will find one enclosed in this letter for you.'
'Please don't send me any money, I have as much as I have time to spend here. Well you cannot get anything here, so the money isn't a lot of good to me. I would rather have the parcel.'

He signed off with his customary short prayer and a birthday kiss for his 'little'uns':

'I must close with sending my best love to you and the kiddies and to all I know. From your loving husband, Jim.'
'God bless you all and may He grant you your wish.'
'PS: give my little Lucy a kiss for me on her birthday.'

This was to be Jim's last letter from 7th Suffolk for some time.

CHAPTER SIX

'...I have been attached to the Royal Engineers...'

LETTER 43

[Wednesday 21 March 1917.
Written to Bertha and the girls.]

An R.E. silk card.

It would seem that on either 19th or 20th March Jim was temporarily attached to the 69th Field Company of the Royal Engineers. The company was also part of 12th 'Eastern' Division and thus Jim was still in the same Arras sector where 7th Suffolk had spent much of the previous five months. Approximately one hundred infantrymen from several different battalions were attached to 69th Field Company at that time, evidently to provide labour for the massive preparations that were underway for the Arras offensive planned for 9th April. According to the 69th Field Company War Diary, the new labour force was largely working with timber:

'Detachment at Le Cauroy Woods felling trees. Detachment at Frévent sawmills. Captain and HQ transport at Lignereuil[1].'

This was vital work as vast amounts of timber were required for a wide variety of purposes including revetting[2] for new and existing trenches, duckboards (as the weather was still wet and cold), ladders for going 'over the top' on 'Z' Day, 9th April and, not least, rough-sawn coffins to cope with the expected casualties.

On 20th March, No. 1 section[3] from Lignereuil and the detachment from Le Cauroy moved to Arras and the following day took up work with the other three sections on artillery preparations. Consequently Jim, who was in good nick at this time, was not a great distance from his battalion:

'....(I am) still better than I have been.'

'...I am not with the battalion at present – I have been attached to the Royal Engineers for a time. I hope I can stop with them. We are billeted close to the battalion so it's not much trouble to go up to see if there is any mail for me. You remember where I am, don't you – remember the views[4] [on the postcards]. I dare say you have had news of the great advance by the British and French[5] – the Allies are gaining ground on every front now, I hope they will keep it up and finish it off so that we can all come back to old Blighty.'

Somehow, Jim had managed to lay his hands on two crucifixes that he sent home for the children; the paper wrapping in which they were sent home still exists, '2 *Crucifixes*' written on the outside:

'I am sending with this letter two crucifixes, one each for the children. I don't know whether it will be in time for Lucy's birthday – I hope it will so you can give it to her with the postcard. If you like them let me know and I will get one for you. You will find in my last letter...four old razor blades[6].

'I wrote to Sid yesterday and thanked him for his kindness to you and the kiddies and I also sent them a postcard. I forgot to tell him I have still got his letter, the one with the Sacred Heart drawn on it. I hope you won't

---

[1] Lignereuil, Le Cauroy and Frevent were hamlets close to the village of Ambrines, where Jim's battalion had been at rest and thus well back from the front line. See map on page 13.

[2] Revetting was timber used to strengthen the trench parapet and parados.

[3] In the RE, the section was the equivalent of the infantry platoon.

[4] This probably referred the Town Hall or the Cathedral in Arras.

[5] This reference is not to the coming Arras offensive but to the German retreat to the massively strong Hindenburg Line. The Germans had not been defeated, they had simply shortened and strengthened their front line. The new line would not be fully breached until late in 1918.

[6] These blades were to be sharpened and returned to Jim.

be vexed, Bertha, but it's the only letter I have kept – I destroy the others after I have read them because I have nowhere to keep them.'

As ever, Jim was concerned about how Bertha could make ends meet and how she could balance work with looking after the children:

'Dear Bertha, I suppose you are getting short of work now. Do you still work for Insley [the name is not clear] because I had a letter from little Ida and she said you were thinking about going to work at the old place, you know where I mean. If you should go there, how will you do with the children?

'God bless you and the children and may He in His mercy grant us peace and bring me back home to you all once again.'

LETTER 44

[Monday 26 March 1917. Written to Bertha and the girls. Address given as – 'Pte. I.J. Elwell, 40659, 7th Suffolks, attached 69th Field Coy, RE, BEF, France.']

Although 69th Field Company War Diary does not make it clear, it appears that Jim remained in and around Arras throughout this period. [In fact, the pages of the war diary that relate to 25th March to 30th March are missing from the record.] Though not far from the Suffolks, Jim had not seen his closest mate for some time:

'Johnny Walker is still safe and well – I don't see him much now, being away from the company.'

The postal service remained a thorn in the side of most soldiers:

'I am sorry to tell you I haven't had a letter from you for nearly (unreadable – smudged) and I haven't received the parcel yet – I am sure that has gone west. How did you send it? By Lazenby[7]? If you did, I shan't give up hope – the other was nearly a month coming. Did you receive the crucifixes safe and the cards too?'

Not knowing what was going on could be extremely irritating, whether it was the uncertainty of items getting through to home or being kept in ignorance of the family's health:

'Tell Mother I will write to her in a day or two. I suppose Nelly has come home again now (from hospital) – I hope she is much better than she has been.

'Did Sid get the letter and card I sent him and how are they all getting on? How is the new baby (Teresa) going? I suppose they make a little bit of a fuss over it. Tell my Nan [most likely Elizabeth Elwell] I have still got the photo. How are Fred and Teresa, your Mother and the others going on? Tell Jim to remember me to all the boys of the fireside. I see we have lost another boy of St. Patrick's, a lad named Killala – I am very sorry.'

The local soldier referred to by Jim was Edward Killala, a lad born in Walsall, who lived at 4, Moat Road and attended St. Patrick's Church in Blue Lane along

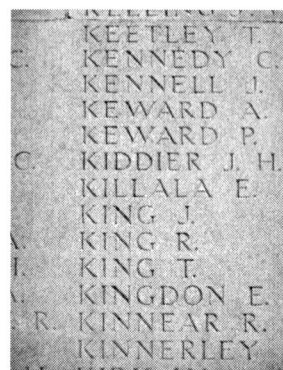

Edward Killala - Thiepval.

with Jim. Edward was just a young lad, making his way as a cutter with J. Shannon and Sons before enlisting in the 10th (Service) Battalion, the Sherwood Foresters in mid-1916. After training, he was shipped out to France on 14th December 1916 and joined his battalion in the line. Through much of that cold, wet winter 17th 'Northern' Division (in which 10th Sherwood Foresters were part of 51st Brigade) had been in and out of the line in the Morval sector of the eastern Somme. On Friday, 4th February, near Saillisel, twenty year-old Edward was killed while on trench-holding duty, probably hit during a German artillery bombardment as his body was never recovered. He is commemorated (see photo above and obituary on page 92) on the huge Thiepval Memorial to the Missing on the ridge above the Ancre Valley. By contrast, two of his brothers served in and survived the war.

Jim signed off in his habitual manner:

'God bless you all and keep you safe and well and bring me back to you all once again.'

---

[7] From Bennett's Business Directory, 1914: 'John W. Lazenby, tourist and excursion organiser and general shipping agent, 51, Park Street, Walsall. L & NW excursion agent. Offices at Brierley Hill.' Lazenby's evidently also shipped parcels out to the Western Front.

LETTER 45

[Saturday 31 March 1917. Written to Bertha and the girls.]

This letter reveals nothing of what Jim and his temporary unit of sappers were doing at the time; to further confuse matters, the Company War Diary pages are also missing:

Sid Powell, c.1916.

'...I am at present in better health than I have been.

'...I am still without a letter....for nearly two weeks. If you can get that swivel hook off Mr. Wood that I asked for I should be very glad. I have written to him and asked about it so perhaps he will give it to you. I have also written to Emmie – she has written me several and this is the first time I have answered them. I have also sent her a postcard.

'...remember me to all I know, also to the men at the Church – there are very few left now, I guess.'

Jim was right about the number of men from St. Patrick's who had become casualties. By the end of the war, the roll of honour for St. Patrick's parish would stand at one hundred and twenty-four killed.

'Well, Dear Bertha, how are they going on in old Blighty? How are Sid and Maria? Did they get the letter and postcard I sent them. I wonder if Maria has started another letter yet – tell her I think she will have lots of time yet before the war is finished. Ask them to let me know how young Siddy is [this is the final reference to young Sid] and to remember me to him when they write.'

When young Sidney Powell (portrait, above) finally was taken into the army he was assigned to 1st Battalion, the Lincolnshire Regiment – no consideration was given to local affiliations, merely to which units were short of men at the time. On finally crossing the Channel, Sid found his battalion with 21st Division, heavily involved in the 3rd Ypres offensive that had commenced on 31st July 1917 and was to grind on, through a campaign notorious for its glutinous mud

and horrific casualty lists, until the second week of November. Sid's part in his first major battle, the Battle of Polygon Wood, began on 29th September and lasted for five days. The following day, 4th October, 21st Division again played a major role in the Battle of Broodseinde, attacking with two brigades at 6 a.m. 1st Lincolnshire was initially held in reserve, though when the lead battalion had crossed the marshy Polygonbeek stream, Sid's battalion advanced into heavy machine gun fire from Judge Copse. Here the teenager was gravely wounded and rapidly sent down the line for treatment. However, two days later, on 6th October, he died in the casualty clearing station and was buried near Ypres in the huge Lijssenthoek Military Cemetery in plot XX. G. 5A. (right). Back home at 29, Newlands Street, Walsall, his parents, Sid and Maria Powell, would have been distraught.

Sid Powell's headstone in Ljissenthoek Cemetery, Belgium.

Yet all of this lay some months in the future; Jim's main present concern was understandably with his children:

'Let me ask you, Dear Bertha, if you and the children are alright? What did they think of the crucifixes and postcards I sent them. I think of them most on Sunday mornings when I used to see them come in Church. I wish I were there to see them again – let us hope, Bertha my girl, that God will grant me that wish soon.

'God bless you all and keep you safe and may He in His mercy grant us peace and bring me safely home to you all once again.'

LETTER 46

[Wednesday 4 April 1917. Written to Bertha and the girls. The address section has been cleanly cut from the top of the page, possibly by the censor.]

69th Field Company War Diary recorded on 3rd April:

'Company ceased work on artillery preparations at 12 noon and moved into cellars [under either the town hall, museum or cathedral].'

On 4th April, the company was:

'Standing to in cellars. Arranging details for operations [that were due to commence on 9th April].'

The cellars referred to in the war diary were part of an impressive system of caverns and tunnels that had been developed, largely by five hundred New Zealand Tunnellers aided by a battalion of Yorkshire 'Bantam'[8] miners, during the six months that preceded the opening of the Battle of Arras on 9th April 1917. Shaken by the losses on the Somme in 1916, the British High Command's intention was to protect many of the battalions going into battle by threading them through tunnels that emerged into the daylight close to the front line. To achieve this, '...a series of subterranean, medieval quarries on the edge of the town (beneath the south eastern suburbs of Ronville and St. Sauveur) would be linked by tunnels to create the most extensive underground network in British military history.'[9] As Robert Hardman points out, 'In a matter of months they (the tunnellers) had created two inter-connected labyrinths, twelve miles long and capable of hiding 25,000 troops.' This underground world was lit by electricity, enjoyed running water, was protected by gas-proof doors and even boasted a 700-bed hospital, several chapels and a sixty-centimetre, light railway. The northerly of the two tunnels, the St. Sauveur Tunnel, ran from the massive Crinchon Sewer (linking the system to the cellars under the Town Hall and the Cathedral) to the front line on the Cambrai Road, to the east of Arras; the more southerly of the tunnels[10], the Ronville Tunnel, ran from the Crinchon Sewer to the front line on the Bapaume Road. This network was accessed from a series of manholes in Arras, the principal ones being located under the town hall, in front of the railway station and beneath the French military barracks, though Robert Hardman comments that the most easily traceable entry is through a basement doorway under a bakery in the Place des Héros (nowadays, it leads only to a cellar). At the other extremity, on the front line, several branch tunnels led via long flights of steps to the surface – a remarkably safe approach to the inevitable dangers of No Man's Land for so many soldiers on 9th April.

Protected by the cellars under the heart of the city, Jim had evidently received the long-awaited parcel and revelled in its contents:

'I have at last received the parcel you posted on 7th March. You couldn't have sent me a better thing than Sheen's[11] – you seem to have known what I did really want. We cannot get it out here and I don't suppose you can get a lot there now but I should not bother to send any more as it must cost you a good deal of money. I have also got what I have been longing for and that is some of your home-made cake. Please don't send me any more handkerchiefs as I have plenty now; I had almost forgotten to thank you for the gloves – they are very good ones, just the right sort.'

The gloves were very welcome as the weather still thought it was mid-winter. Jim sent on his regards to his friends and his love to his family:

'Remember me to all I know, your sisters and brothers, your Mother too.
'Let me close with sending my best love to you and the children; are they good little girls now? I hope so. Let me wish you, Bertha, a very happy Easter time.
'God bless you and the children and keep you safe and bring me back home to you and all once again.'
'PS: Dear Bertha, please send some fags as we cannot get them now.'

It seems from what Jim said that the frequent handouts of cigarettes and tobacco that had characterised his early days in the army had come to an abrupt end. Soldiers could put up with most things if they had the two staples of the trench soldier – strong tea and cigarettes.

LETTER 47
[Thursday 5 April 1917. Written to Bertha and the girls.]

The following day [5 April, 'V' Day, four days prior to the offensive] in the same caves and cellars under Arras, Jim had plenty of time on his hands, writing two letters on this occasion. In the first, he took the opportunity to reply at length to Bertha's letter that had arrived that morning:

'....in answer to your kind and welcome letter – it has been such a long time since I had one. I'm glad you received the crosses safely but you didn't say if you would like one but you know what they say – silence gives consent, so I will try to get one for you.'

[8] 'Bantams' were soldiers below the Army's prescribed minimum height of 5 feet 3 inches.
[9] Quoted from Robert Hardman's article in the Daily Mail on 15th March 2008, 'City Under the Slaughter.'
[10] One of the caverns in this sector, 'La Carrière Wellington', is now open to the public after eighteen years' hard endeavour, thanks largely to M. Alain Jacques, head of the Arras Archaeology Department and M. Jean-Marie Prestaux, Director of Tourism in Arras.
[11] T.C. Sheen was a bakery at 68, Park Street, Walsall, making speciality cakes and loaves.

'I dare say our little Lucy would swank a little on her birthday, especially when she got the postcards and crosses I sent her. I sent Lizzie one because I knew how she would take it if I didn't.'

'If you go to work again where you did before, who's going to look after the kiddies? Then again, Bertha, if you should go home with (my) Mother, what about the things? Where would you put those? Mind you, I would rather be on our own but if it's going to do you and the old folks any good I shall say, "by all means, go." If God spares me to come home again I shall be content to live anywhere or anyhow but thank God I do know this, you and the kiddies will have a good home, so let me ask you to decide. If you choose not to go and don't like to tell Mother let me know and I will write and let them all know.'

Bertha's letter spoke of some kind of bad news from Jim's former place of employment:

'I was very surprised to hear that news about Marson but between you and me I was always very suspicious of him, in fact I never trusted him with any of my secrets; Bailey never would either. And poor old Freddie Wood – he's a good sort, as you say.'

No details were forthcoming and one might only speculate on what indiscretion the man had committed.

Jim signed off in his usual manner:

'God bless you all and keep you safe and well and bring me back home to you and all once again.'

LETTER 48
[Thursday 5 April 1917. The only surviving letter to his Mother and Dad.]

The second letter that Jim wrote on 5th April suggests that he and the R.E.'s in the caverns and tunnels under the city were simply waiting for time to pass. Logically, much of that time was devoted to the perennial letter-writing – after all, a man could never know whether a letter was to be his last. Of the letters that Jim wrote to his parents, this is the only one to survive and, like most front-line soldiers, he was quick to tell them that he was well:

'….this letter leaves me a treat to what I have been.

'I can't tell you a lot….I am alright and that's about all. I don't see Johnny Walker now, you see I have moved from him but the last I heard of him he was still going strong (with 7th Suffolk). By the way, did you both get the cards I sent you? Please let me know in your next letter.

'I have at last received the parcel from Bertha that was sent on 7th March…..thanks very much dear Mother and Dad for your share and also thank Nell for her share too. Well, Mother, I am very sorry to say I have not received a letter from you for a long time now, nor from Bertha either. I think they have all got lost.

'Well, Mother, will you please ask our Bertha if she will kindly get me some fags and send them on to me. We cannot get them out here now like we used to do. I wrote to her yesterday but forgot to ask her about the fags. Poor old girl, she will think I am on the beg all the time but I can't do without a smoke.'

Jim's comments confirm that cigarettes were the one thing that made life anything like bearable at the front. The news that brother Ted had again been home on leave must have made Jim wonder about the fairness of a system that often left men without home leave for more than a year [in fact, Jim was never granted leave]:

'I was glad to hear Ted had been on leave again – I dare say you were all pleased to see him once again. I wish I could, as well. Has Tom [Spencer, Rose's husband] gone yet or did he get a further exemption? I hope he did.'

The exemption that Tom Spencer enjoyed might have been assessed as necessary on account of his job, family circumstances, health or some other basis. Jim signed off as usual:

'Let me close by sending my best love to all my sisters and brothers and accept the same yourselves. From your loving son, Jim.

'God be with you till we meet again. Let us pray that God in His mercy will soon grant us peace that we can all meet once again.' [Signed with a kiss for Mother].

LETTER 49
[Saturday 7 April 1917. Written to Bertha and the girls.]

At time of writing this letter (7th April, 'X' Day), Jim was still with the Royal Engineers in the caves and cellars under the centre of Arras and, though it was safe, the men could hear and feel the percussive effects of the massive artillery bombardment that was raining down on the German lines:

'We are having it pretty warm here now, I mean in war not in weather. I dare say you know that by reading the papers. It was at one time a very cushy place here but it's livened up a lot just lately. Our people are trying now to smash up Old Fritz on this front – I hope they will soon do it and get the thing over. I am still the same as the views; you understand, Bertha, don't you?'

The reference to '...the views' was telling Bertha to look at the picture postcards that Jim had sent in previous months, probably showing Arras town hall or cathedral. Jim, however, was still in seventh heaven over the most recent parcel to arrive from his wife:

'I enjoyed the contents of your parcel immensely – you could not have sent me a better thing than Sheen's; also the butter and cheese. (In future) please don't waste your money on sweets or fruits of any kind; I would much rather have the same as you sent before if you can possibly get it. I know it's difficult now the prices are so high but if it is only one now and again I should be quite satisfied. You know what I mean by Sheen's, don't you? I must tell you this, Bertha old girl, I enjoyed that butter (more) than I did the cake. The B [unidentified] was alright too. I want you to send me....fags as we cannot get them here now for any money. I dare say, Bertha, you will think I am always begging off you but I am like Father Mac(Donell) – he don't know how to beg but he has got a very good way of asking his people which always seems to get a splendid response.'

Having stated several times previously that he was comfortable for money, Jim ironically now found that he was struggling for funds at a time when he desperately wanted to send a present home:

'Dear Bertha, I cannot send the crucifix this time as I promised you as....the funds are very low at present but you shall have one, Bertha my girl, if it costs me my last penny.'

Jim added a timely reminder about the swivel hook that he needed to clip to his belt to secure his clasp knife:

'I haven't had the swivel hook yet – I suppose it will be coming along soon now.'

He ended his letter in his habitual fashion:

'Now, Dear Bertha, let me ask you to remember me to all I know and let me send to you and my little'uns my very best love. From your loving husband, Jim'
    'God bless you all and keep you safe and bring me safely home to you all once again.'

On 9th April, 'Z' Day, the waiting ceased for thousands of British and Empire troops as the main infantry attack went in, both on Vimy Ridge and in front of Arras. As Robert Hardman explains, 'When the time came, at 5:30 a.m. on April 9th 1917, Easter Monday, the British Third Army marched down their exit tunnels, up their designated stairwells and out into the open.' The engineers, under the direction of 35th Brigade, had been allotted specific tasks that were dependent upon the infantry capturing enemy trenches; their tasks included the construction of strong points at Feuchy Chapelle [one of the initial objectives of 35th Brigade], building a tramway from the cemetery at Arras towards Feuchy Chapel, labelling captured German trenches and making a pack animal track across German lines. At 6 a.m. the sections moved off to their assembly places near the front line via the complex of cellars and tunnels.

However, two days later Jim's stay with the engineers came to an abrupt end, as the RE Company War Diary for 11th April recorded:

'About 10 a.m. orders were received to return the 100 infantry attached for work to their battalions.'

Jim did not send another headed letter until 22nd April, by which time he had long since returned to his old battalion. During the time that Jim had been attached to the Royal Engineers, 7th Suffolk had lost twenty-five men killed and many more wounded, injured or ill. Nevertheless, he was probably glad to be back with his mates.

CHAPTER SEVEN
'Back with the old battalion...'

On 11th April, **the day** that Jim Elwell returned to his battalion, 7th Suffolk was in the front line until **11:30 p.m.** when relieved by 11th Middlesex; the **battalion** moved back to Feuchy Chapelle and then **into reserve**. At half past midnight on the 13th, the **Suffolks** were again relieved and marched into rest **billets** at the Oil Factory in Arras (north of the Scarpe and between St Nicholas and St. Laurent-Blangy – see map on page 13) where the men were given the chance to clean themselves and their equipment – it was desperately needed as the unit had been in action intermittently since zero hour on 9th April. At 8:20 a.m. on 14th April, the battalion set out to march the six or so miles west to Wanquetin, arriving there at 11:45 a.m. Billets were pronounced to be *'good.'* Having not written for a week, Jim took the opportunity of the brief respite to dash off a field postcard to let Bertha know he was okay.

FIELD SERVICE POSTCARD 50
[Monday 14 April 1917. Written to Bertha.]

All Jim was allowed to say, by the 'delete as applicable' process, was:

'I am quite well.
'I have received your letter.
'Letter follows at first opportunity.'

The following day they moved west yet again, this time on to Halloy, a village just short of the town of Doullens; the men started at 6:45 a.m. and arrived at 1:15 p.m. to be billeted in a proper camp – a rare luxury! During the afternoon a much-needed draft of 127 men and one officer arrived. The lads might have thought that they were up for a period of rest but next morning they were disabused of that idea as training began in earnest. After two days at work, the battalion moved east, back to Fosseux (near Wanquetin) for a day, then a mile further on to Gouy-en-Artois where again they were billeted in huts. Four more days of intensive training then commenced on 20th April – the old hands suspected, rightly, that the battalion's part in the Arras offensive was not yet over.

LETTER 51
[Sunday 22 April 1917. Final full letter from Jim to Bertha and the girls. Headed, '14 Platoon, 'D' Coy, 7th Suffolk, BEF, France.']

It was from the billet in Gouy-en-Artois that Jim wrote what was to be his last full letter (below) to Bertha and the girls, on Sunday, 22nd April:

'Dear Bertha, Just a few lines hoping to find you and the kiddies in the best of health which it leaves me at present. I am glad to tell you we are doing a little better now than we were doing when I wrote you my last letter. We are both alright, me and Johnny Walker. I was sorry to hear of young Smith being reported missing – they seem to be going off one at a time from the Church. I suppose there is but a few left now. I shall thank God when it is all over.'

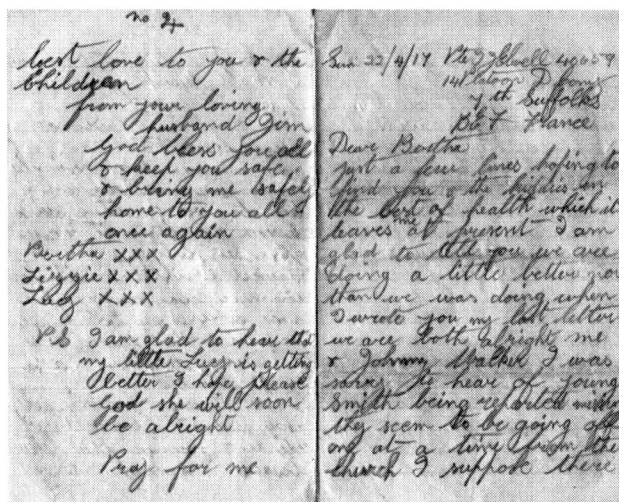

Jim Elwell's final letter to his wife Bertha and his 'Little'uns, 22nd April 1917

The *'...young Smith'* that Jim wrote about might have been Charles Smith who is commemorated in Walsall on the Parish Roll of Honour in St. Patrick's Roman Catholic Church – more likely, since no records refer to Charles Smith as having died in early 1917, *'young Smith'* had been taken prisoner and would survive the war.

During the previous few days Jim had received at least four letters:

'Dear Bertha, I have had a letter from Maria, one from Emmie and one from Charlie Neville (Jim's brother-in-law). I have not got the time to answer them yet so if you see them, thank them for their letters and tell them I will write to them the first chance I get. Oh, by the way, will you thank my Mother and Dad for theirs too – give my best love to them all.'

'Dear Bertha, I don't quite understand you with the 'x'; please try to explain it better to me in your next letter. Please let me ask you to forgive me for being so long in replying to your letter and also let me thank you for the fags I received the other night. They came just in time; I was out of them so it was a bit of luck for me.'

Jim's letter must have reached home quickly because in a letter from Bertha dated 29th April (one that was later returned to her – see letter 56 on pages 73-74) she wrote:

'Dear Jim, you ask me what 'x' means – well, Jim, I told you that you would always find money where that was. If I must send you some more money I shall put it in a box of fags with an 'x' on so you will know.'

It is almost as if Jim had had a premonition that this would be his last goodbye as it was more protracted than ever before:

'And now, Dear Bertha, I haven't any more to tell you so let me conclude my letter by sending my best love to you and the children. From your loving husband, Jim.
    God bless you all and keep you safe and bring me safely home to you all once again.
    Bertha xxx
    Lizzie xxx
    Lucy xxx

PS: I am glad to hear that my little Lucy is getting better. I hope, please God, she will soon be alright. Pray for me.'

7th Suffolk completed its training on 23rd April. The Battalion War Diary recorded:

'24th April - 7:20 a.m. Moved by bus to Arras. Billeted in Museum Cellars and Crypt (of the Cathedral). 25th April - moved to Railway Triangle (see map 3 on page 69) at 4:15 a.m. Took over from 17th Division and took over front line in the evening. Details (of men) left in Arras. Left Railway Triangle at 8:20 p.m. and went into support. Relieved (10th) West Yorkshires, 17th Division. 26th and 27th April - remained in support; fairly quiet.'

'In support' meant that Jim's battalion was in the rear trenches, positioned so that it could be quickly moved up if the enemy launched a counter-offensive. Jim probably wrote his final field postcard while huddled in a dugout, hoping that the card would set the family's mind at rest as he had not written home for five days.

FIELD SERVICE POSTCARD 52
[Friday 27 April 1917.
Written to Bertha.]

This last field service postcard (below) was postmarked 'Field Post Office, 5th May', exactly a week after Jim was killed.

Jim's final field service postcard.

It read as follows:

'I am quite well.'
    'Letter follows at first opportunity.'
    'I have received no letter from you lately.'
    'I J Elwell.'

The field postcard, Jim's final communication from France, appears to have been hastily written, probably just after the battalion had been informed that it was to go 'over the top' in the morning....

THE BATTLE OF ARLEUX, 28th-29th APRIL 1917

According to Scott and Brumwell in the *'History of the 12th Division'*, the Division took position:

'...on that portion of the front extending from the north east corner of Monchy (le Preux) to the River Scarpe [see map 3 on page 69]'.

MAP THREE The Arras sector – 7th Suffolk (35th Brigade, 12th 'Eastern' Division) attack, 28th April 1917

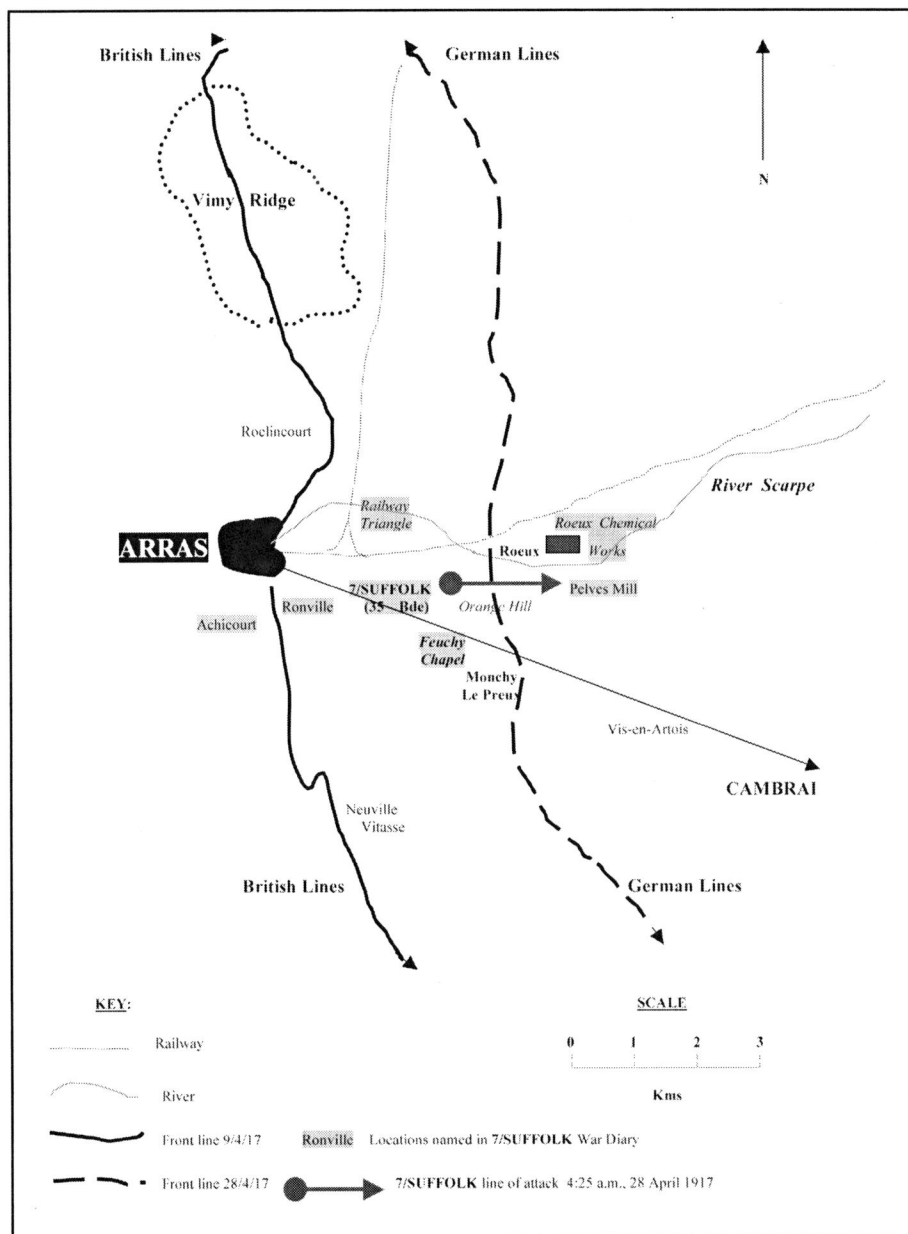

Berkshires and capture the second objective of Pelves Mill. Zero hour was set for 4:25 a.m., thus it was still dark when Jim and his mates heard rather than saw the two lead battalions rise from their trenches to venture into No Man's Land. Immediately, 7th Norfolk's left wing companies were hammered by machine guns from Rifle Trench that had been almost untouched by the preparatory artillery barrage; however, the Norfolks' right wing companies courageously took the far end of Rifle Trench and made for their next objective at 5:45 a.m. but they too were stopped dead by machine guns. To the left of the Norfolks, 5th Royal Berkshire stormed the whole of Bayonet Trench as far as the River Scarpe and also took a short section of Rifle Trench, preparing the way for 7th Suffolk to pass through and strike for their final objective of Pelves Mill. In the rising light of a surprisingly mild day, 7th Suffolk left their trenches and, deploying into artillery formation[1], found and passed through the Berkshires. As Jim's battalion breasted the ridge of Orange Hill and began a long, downhill trek with the River Scarpe sparkling on their left, they walked into a heavy German defensive barrage rendered near impenetrable by murderous machine gun fire from the direction of the uncaptured village of Roeux and so were forced to take refuge in shell holes and dead ground. The surviving officers rallied the men for another '...gallant effort' (a description given in the 'Official History, France & Belgium, 1917 volume one') to reach the distant Pelves Mill but the lack of cover and sheer weight of enemy fire kept them at bay as the butcher's bill rose alarmingly – by the end of the day, every one of 7th Suffolk's officers except the C.O. and the Adjutant had become casualties along with eighty-nine other ranks

In the attack, one that was to coincide with an attempt by 34th and 37th Divisions north of the Scarpe to capture Roeux in preparation for the main attack that would go in a week later on 3rd May, the first objective of 35th Brigade was the northern section of Bayonet Trench and the section of Rifle Trench from the Monchy-Pelves Mill Road; the second objective was Pelves Mill itself, south of the River Scarpe from Roeux. Thus the capture of Roeux by 34th and 37th Divisions was pivotal to the success of 35th Brigade – without it, the attack would be doomed from the outset. The assault was to go in with 7th Norfolk on the right, 5th Royal Berkshire on the left and 7th Suffolk to pass through the

[1] 'Artillery formation' meant advancing in small units, such as platoons or sections, in narrow columns of fours or even in file, thus presenting a minimal target for enemy artillery.

killed or missing with many more wounded. Despite its sterling efforts, the battalion had made little progress beyond Bayonet Trench and Rifle Trench. One survivor later said:

'The opposition was more than we expected and we lost heavily. The wounded and the dead were brought away as far as possible.'

Another stated quite plainly:

'The ground was lost and we had to retire – the time was awful.'

Other survivors spoke of:

'....many fatal wounds from shrapnel just in front of our trenches.
'....men caught by shells in the open, on top of the ridge (Orange Hill) and in the advance from the Sunken Road towards Monchy.
'....shells (were) also falling on the way to the dressing station.'

Such was the punishment taken by the battalion that it was withdrawn from the line on 29th April and the remaining men were reorganised into just two very weak companies. While 36th and 37th Brigades of 12th

Division stayed in the line and continued the assault, 35th Brigade came out of the line and into reserve to lick its wounds. It had just fought in what became known to posterity as the Battle of Arleux, named after a village well to the north of the River Scarpe.

At some time during the maelstrom it appears that Jim had been slightly wounded and had evidently made his way back to the Regimental Aid Post. This is confirmed by the initial card (below, left) sent by the Infantry Record Office, No.9 District, Warley on 15th May 1917, informing Bertha that Jim Elwell had been:

'Slightly wounded in action on 28th April 1917.'

However, on 14th June this message was amended by a second card from the same office that now indicated that Jim had been:

'.... posted as missing and wounded on 28/4/17.' (see notification below).

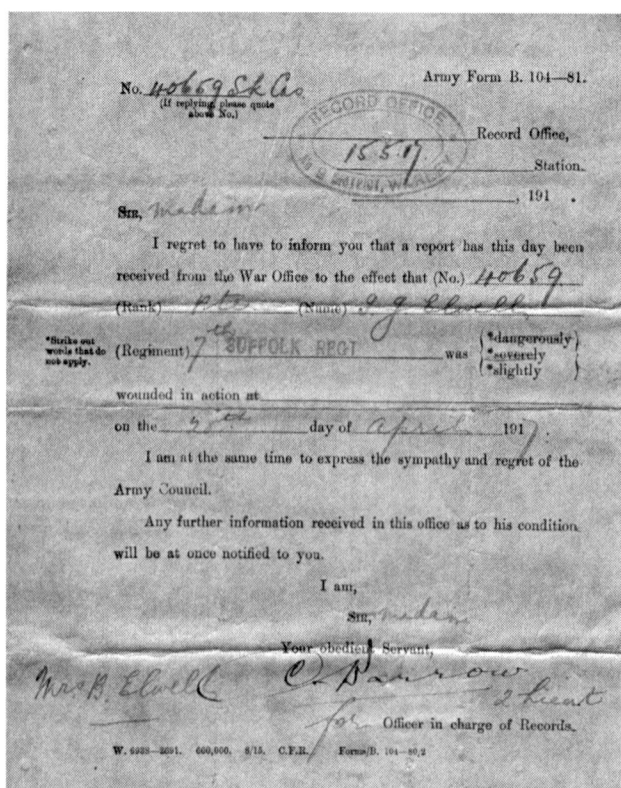

The second casualty letter, '...missing and wounded.'

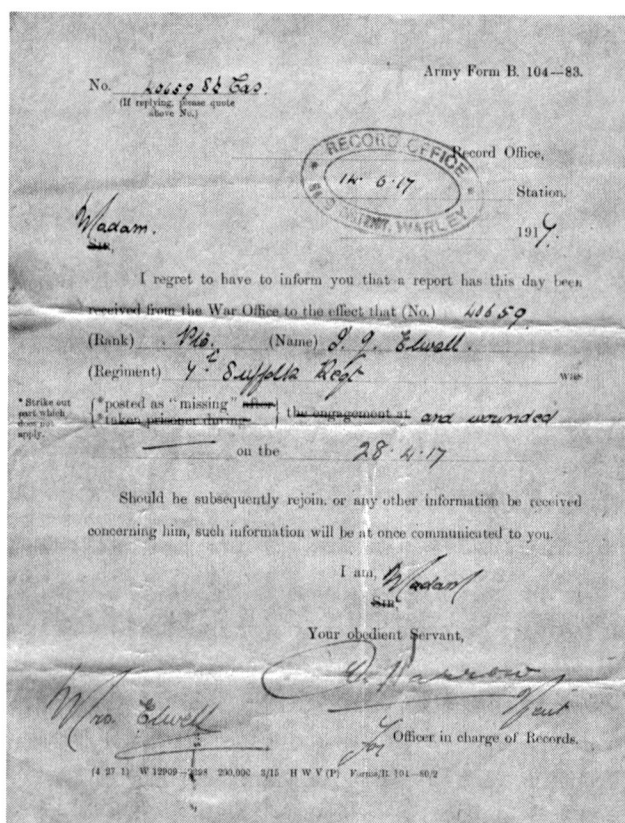

The first casualty letter, ' ...slightly wounded.'

The situation on 28th April on Orange Hill, as on any battlefield, had been very confused. What precisely had befallen Jim will never be ascertained beyond doubt but by piecing together the few known facts, by reading between the lines and by adding a degree of speculation we may come close to what happened. The '...*slightly wounded'* statement is unambiguous; it is highly likely that Jim was seen by one of his mates when he was hit as friends tended to go into action together. A slight wound would have meant that Jim, as 'walking wounded', very probably made his own way back to the Regimental Aid Post and once there he would most certainly have been recognised and recorded. Let us now assume that, after receiving first aid, it was decided to send Jim down the line for further treatment; this would have been done by moving 'walking wounded' and stretcher cases through the communication trenches and loading them into horse-drawn or motor wagons that served as ambulances and then transporting the men to the nearest Casualty Clearing Station, possibly at Frévent to the west of Arras.

The next problem to resolve is how *'...slightly wounded'* became *'..wounded and missing'*; usually, a man was posted as 'missing in action' as a result of being hit directly by artillery fire or buried by a near miss. Equally, a man might be killed by rifle or machine gun fire in No Man's Land; if the attack in which he was taking part was unsuccessful and the front lines remained where they already were, then a man might lie between the trench lines for many months. Numerous subsequent artillery duels churned over the same ground so that when the battlefield was eventually 'cleared', there was no means of identifying many of the men who had died in earlier battles. Yet in Jim's case, none of the previous possibilities apply as he was almost certainly back inside battalion lines. Now it is important to remember what was happening in the battle; the German artillery was not only laying down a heavy defensive barrage in front of, and on, the men who were attacking their trench lines but also on the British support lines and rear areas in order to prevent reinforcements from being brought forward to increase the pressure of the attack. It is not beyond possibility that one of these German shells registered a direct hit on the ambulance or stretcher-bearers transporting Jim to what he thought was safety. Unfortunately, direct hits leave little more than a huge crater, accounting for Jim being reported 'missing'.

Months, and ultimately years, of uncertainty and anxiety mixed with nagging hope had thus begun for Bertha.

Notes on Walsall men killed serving with 7th Suffolk on 28th April 1917:

Jim was not the only Walsall lad to be killed with 7th Suffolk in the attack of 28th April 1917 down Orange Hill towards Pelves Mill. Four lads who were transferred from 1/6th South Staffordshire to 7th Suffolks at the end of September 1916 were also killed, named as follows:-

40581, **Private Harry Birch** *of Victor Street, Caldmore, Walsall.*
Commemorated on bay 4 of the Arras Memorial to the Missing.

40596, **Private John Thomas Dickinson** *of Frederick Street, Walsall.*
Buried plot V. F. 9 of Feuchy Chapel British Cemetery, Wancourt.

40652, **Private Arthur Ross** *of Cemetery Road, Bloxwich.*
Commemorated on bay 4 of the Arras Memorial to the Missing.

40593, **Lance-Corporal Albert Stych, M.M.,** *of Parker Street, Bloxwich.*
Commemorated on bay 4 of the Arras Memorial to the Missing.

Jim Elwell's best mate, Alf 'Johnny' Walker survived not only the Battle of Arleux but also the rest of the war and returned home to Walsall.
[Most of the information on these lads was kindly furnished by Graeme Clarke who has taken on the massive task of researching all of the Walsall men who died in the Great War.]

CHAPTER EIGHT
'Aftermath – wounded and missing...'

(i) Bertha's Returned Letters

In the weeks following 28th April, Bertha received back four letters that she had sent to Jim that had not arrived before he went into action for the final time. The

A returned letter – 'wounded, present location unknown.'

envelope in which they were sent home, (shown above), originally addressed by Bertha to '69th Field Company' and post-marked '18th April 1917' [thus it was probably the envelope for letter 54 on pages 72-73], bears the handwritten word *'wounded'* in pencil and an official stamp *'present location uncertain'*. It thus confirms that Jim was definitely wounded and missing but adds nothing to the explanation. A second instance of returned items, quite unheralded, came out of the blue almost a year later, in April 1918, from a complete stranger who lived in Gloucestershire. This time, it would provide a direct link to Jim.

LETTER 53
[Sunday 8 April 1917.
Written by Bertha to Jim (returned).]

This letter from Bertha reflects the contents of Jim's previous letters:

'....we are all in the pink, as you say.'

'I do hope, Jim, that you do not deceive me about being well.'

'Have you had two parcels yet? If not, I should tell Alf to keep them for you or else tell them to bring them where you are [Bertha assumed, as she had been told no differently, that Jim was still attached to the Royal Engineers].

'Oh, if this war would only end and you could come home I would not care so much...it is cruel to be here all by myself. I sit hour after hour and unless Maria or MaryAnn (Bertha's sisters) comes across I never see anyone after I come out of the shop.

'I have had all the postcards and the two crucifixes – they are grand. I am going to buy the two children two silver chains when I do a full week's work. Our boss did not get that order...before Christmas, but he has an order for 6,000 head collars so....I start on full time this Easter Monday (the next day). I have got Mrs Partridge to look after Lizzie for me.

'We had an aeroplane accident up Ryecroft and a woman from the Church and a child were killed. Father Mac gave it out – her name was North.

'Young Sid (Powell) went last week.

'Have you had your swivel (hook) yet – I sent it you in a letter about five or six weeks ago.

'Best love from Maria, Sid and family, and MaryAnn and Jim.

'May Jesus, Mary and Joseph watch over you and protect you from all danger and bring you back safe home again to us all.'

LETTER 54
[Tuesday 17 April 1917. Written
by Bertha to Jim (returned).]

The second of Bertha's returned letters continued in the same vein:

'I received three letters in one day.

'Our boss has got a very large order – we are working till 9 o'clock at night and 5 o'clock on Saturday and he wants us to put more time in.

'I have sent Lizzie to Mrs. G. Partridge and of course I get Lucy ready and send her to Maria, so it's only bed and work for me but I don't mind that as long as I can get some money for when you come home.

'I have made up my mind to keep my home as it is, for the summer at any rate, to see if you are coming home for Christmas. If you have got to stop out there another winter I shall not stick another winter on my own. I shall ask your Mother to let us stay there till you come home then I shall get a house and get it ready for you as soon as I know you are coming.

'Jim, if you are short (of money) why don't you let me send you some? Do you get any extra for being in the RE [he should have done] because I was told I should get more money but it has made no difference to my money yet. I am sending you a parcel – I am sending (it with) Laz(enby) because it is the cheapest way to send to you, Jim.

'May Jesus, Mary and Joseph watch over you and protect you from all danger and bring you back safe home again. Good night and may God bless you with His mercy.'

LETTER 55
[Thursday 19 Apr 1917. Written by Bertha to Jim (returned).]

The third of these letters shows that Bertha had recently sent Jim an excellent parcel; it is more than likely that his mates shared the bounty after Jim failed to return. This was the typical Tommy taking the practical view that it was a shame to let good food and cigarettes go to waste:

'I was very sorry to hear about you not having any money – you will find a little inside this letter. Your parcel will contain a cake….bread, some butter, cheese, chocolate, one dozen Woodbines, one box of Players (off Ada Peabody) and a brown loaf. I will send you some bread and butter also cheese every week – after this you shan't go hungry. (When you receive a parcel) always keep as much as you can for yourself to keep your strength up.

'I wonder when this cruel war will end. I do hope, please God, it won't be long now. Our Sid has had a mass said for you this week and I am going to have one said for you next week, so you see, Jim, someone thinks about you and longs to see you come back safe

again. Do try to keep your head down when you go to fight for it must be cruel for you.'

Given what was to occur a week later, this paragraph above represents a harsh irony.

'I was sorry to hear you going out of the RE's – I wish they would keep you in it.'

'May Jesus, Mary and Joseph watch over you and protect you from all danger and bring you back safe to me and the children.'

LETTER 56
[Sunday 29 Apr 1917. Final letter from Bertha to Jim (returned).]

Bertha's final letter was written the day after Jim had been killed and contains one remarkable near-premonition of Jim's death:

'…glad to know you are a bit better.

'I sent you 3 shillings[1] in my registered letter, I hope you get it safe; it was 1s. from me, 1s. from your Mother and 1s. from my Mother.

'My Mother is sending you a tart. She says that she knows you would enjoy it as it has been a long time since you had one of hers.'

'Dear Jim, you ask me what 'x' means – well, Jim, I told you that you would always find money where that was. If I must send you some more money I shall put it in a box of fags with an 'x' on so you will know.'

'Dear Jim, I had such a fright on April 28th. I never saw you more plainly in my life. You came to the side of my bed and when I jumped up in bed you went. It did make me feel bad; it was at a quarter to six. I could not sleep after so I got up and went to Church at 8 o'clock. I do wish it had been true but I must be patient. God knows best when this war will end. Your Mother tells me that Ted (Elwell) is joining our Church and Nell told me that your Mother seems as pleased as he is.

'I saw Mr. Wood and he told me that he was going to send you a small parcel. And Sid wants to know if you have had the cards that they sent you in Maria's letter. Young Bertha [Sid and Maria's daughter] sent you one - if you get a chance send her a postcard. She will think such a lot of it.

---

[1] One old shilling was the equivalent of 5p. It was, of course, worth so much more in 1917.

'May Jesus, Mary and Joseph watch over you and protect you from all danger and bring you back safe home to us all.'

Little did Bertha know it but this chilling premonition was the closest she would ever come to seeing her husband again.

(ii)   Fighting Bureaucracy

To be informed that a loved one was 'missing' was the cruellest of all outcomes. 'Wounded' always gave hope that a man would return to England and possibly recover his health to a certain extent. 'Killed in action', devastating as it was in its finality, at the very least afforded a man's relatives and friends the opportunity to grieve for him. 'Missing' put the lives of those back home into limbo – they couldn't grieve but neither could they expect him home; all that was left was to hope against hope that a man had been captured and to clutch at every straw that drifted by. Such was Bertha's fate.

LETTER 57
*[15 May 1917. From the Infantry
Record Office, Warley.]*

On 15th May 1917, Bertha received the much dreaded but official 'wound notification card' (see page 70) informing her that Jim had been:

'*...slightly wounded in action on 28th April 1917.*' It bore the origin, '*Infantry Record Office, No.9 District, Warley*'.

By return post, Bertha requested more information, though the letter she sent (letter 58, below) was not in her own hand.

LETTER 58
*[Undated but about 17 May 1917. Written on
behalf of Bertha to the Infantry Record Office, No.9
District, Warley.]*

'Dear Sir, since receiving your communication dated May 15th last informing me my husband.....was wounded (slightly) on April 28th, I have not received any further news of him. Will you please inform me whether you have any further record of him or could

you tell me where he now is that I may write to him. Thanking you in anticipation.

I am, Yours truly,

Mrs. B. Elwell'

LETTERS 59 AND 60
*[19 May and 14 June 1917 from the
Infantry Records Office, Warley.]*

On 19th May, Bertha received a reply from the Infantry Record Office stating that there was no further information. However, on 14th June that same office sent a card (see page 70) bearing the amended and chilling message that Jim had been:

'*....posted as **missing** (author's emphasis) and wounded on 28/4/17.*'

This prompted Bertha to write to the British Red Cross Enquiry Department for Wounded and Missing in London.

LETTER 61
*[26 June 1917 from the
War Office, London.]*

The reply came from the War Office and baldly stated:

'In reply to your enquiry addressed to the British Red Cross Society....Private I.J. Elwell is officially reported as wounded and missing since the 28th April 1917. Further enquiries to be addressed to the Infantry Record Office, St. Brelades, Warley Mount, Warley.'

The bureaucrats were at work. In desperation, Bertha turned to a politician, writing to the Liberal party's prospective parliamentary candidate for Walsall, Mr. W.H. Brown, who replied promptly and kindly in the following terms.

LETTER 62
*[Wednesday, 15 July 1917. Written by W.H. Brown, to
Bertha on notepaper headed – 'Walsall Liberal Association
– Mr W.H. Brown, Springfield, Queens Road,
Leytonstone.']*

'I am sorry to hear that Private Elwell is officially reported to be 'missing'. I am puzzling my brains to see if I can assist at all. I have correspondents in nearly all the prison camps in Germany and I will write to ask any news of him.

'Trusting your agony of suspense may soon be terminated by the best of good news.

Yours etc, W.H. Brown.'

LETTER 63

[20 June 1917 from the Regimental Paymaster, Warley.]

Mr. Brown's reference to *'prison camps'* in letter 62 would have revived Bertha's expectations but whatever the truth of Jim's disappearance and however excruciating the pain, Bertha and the children still needed a regular income, so the arrival of the standard letter in respect of Separation Allowance was welcome despite the implicit reminder it carried:

Private I.J. Elwell

'From the Regimental Paymaster, Warley, 20th June 1917. (Since Pte. I. J. Elwell has been reported missing).... Separation Allowance and Allotment will continue for a period of 30 weeks from the above date, up to 13th January 1918. To enable payment please return (your) identity certificate; it will be returned for next week. [The certificate was evidently required to be produced at the counter each week to obtain payment.]'

Thus another heartrending dilemma, one that would not be resolved for two months, now presented itself – what, if anything, should be written in the local newspaper? The eventual solution was straightforward; simply report Jim as, *'wounded and missing.'* This was done in time for the *'Walsall Observer'* edition of Saturday, 28th July 1917 when a photograph (see page above) and the following report appeared:

'Private I.J. Elwell is reported to be wounded and missing. Thirty-eight years of age [actually he was thirty-seven] and married with two children, he was employed before joining the Suffolk Regiment in June 1916 [he actually joined the South Staffordshire in this

month, transferring to the Suffolks in September 1916] by Mr. Jagger of Green Lane. His home is at 42, Blue Lane West.'

LETTER 64

[8 August 1917 from the Infantry Record Office, Warley.]

In view of the fact that the Separation Allowance was of limited duration, on 8th August the Infantry Record Office sent Bertha the necessary pro-forma (Army Form B. 104-106) to enable her to claim a pension. It had to be filled in:

'...and subscribed before a magistrate.'

She was advised to return the form along with her marriage certificate and the birth certificates of Lizzie and Lucy. The pension would then be issued:

'...after 30 weeks of Separation Allowance from the date she was informed husband was missing.'

LETTER 65

[5 September 1917 from the Ministry of Pensions.]

The Ministry of Pensions (Widows and Dependants Branch) duly returned the certificates on 5th September. The next letter that Bertha received was considerably more welcome.

LETTER 66

[Wednesday, 12 December 1917. Written by Alf Walker to his cousin, Bertha.]

This letter came from Bertha's cousin, and Jim's best mate, Alf 'Johnny' Walker and his letter makes it clear that, having been either ill or wounded, he was expecting any day to be returned to the front line. He did not know whether he would go back to 7th Suffolk or be posted to a different battalion when he reached France:

'Don't you think of sending me any money for those beads – if you do I shall be offended. (I will get your sister some beads) ...if I have gone up the line again I will get them as soon as I can. I am marked 'A' again but I don't know when I shall be going, it may be months, it may be days. You never know with the Army.

'Sorry to hear about Aunt Martha [Jim's mother]. I went to see her when I was over – my word, she was nothing but a frame. [Probably an extreme reaction to Jim's loss six months earlier]. I felt sorry for her.

'Well, cousin, have you heard any more about Jim? I never see any of our old chums but if I go back to my old battalion I may get to know more if any of the old boys are there.

'Remember me to the children and tell them I shall be coming to see them again soon. Good night and God bless you. Remember me to your mother.'

For Bertha the letter would have seemed bittersweet; it was good to hear from her cousin but it was a stark reminder of Jim, who had so often written of Alf in his letters.

LETTER 67

[Friday, 4th January 1918. Written by the Ministry of Pensions to Bertha.]

For once everything on the financial front proceeded smoothly and on 4th January 1918 the pension authorities again contacted Bertha:

'I am directed by the Minister of Pensions to inform you that the issue of your Separation Allowance will cease on 13th January and that you have been awarded a pension of 13/9d a week for yourself and an allowance of 9/2d a week for your two children, with effect from 14th January.

'The pension will be payable weekly in advance through the Post Office, as in the case of Separation Allowance, but on Wednesdays instead of Mondays. The first payment will be made on 16th January 1918.

'The enclosed forms of Life Certificate should be carefully completed....and returned to this office as soon as possible. If not returned within eight days the payment of the pension may be delayed.'

Yet the letter advised Bertha that:

'The change of payment must not be taken as indicating that there is any proof of the death of your husband.'

Evidently even the army thought that Jim might just possibly still be alive, so the painful confusion continued for Bertha and the family.

LETTER 68

[Monday, 8th January 1918. Written to Bertha by the Pensions Issue Office, Baker Street, London.]

This next pensions memorandum, necessary though it was, showed the bureaucrats in full spate, stating that:

'....payment of your pension, weekly in advance from the 14th January has been authorised to be made at the Post Office named by you. A certificate of identity is enclosed. A life certificate will be required from you each quarter....in order that further issues of your pension may be authorised.

W.F. Shannon,
    Superintendent.'

LETTER 69

[Thursday, 8th March 1918. Written by the British Red Cross to Bertha.]

Two months later, on 8th March, the British Red Cross contacted Bertha (below) to inform her that:

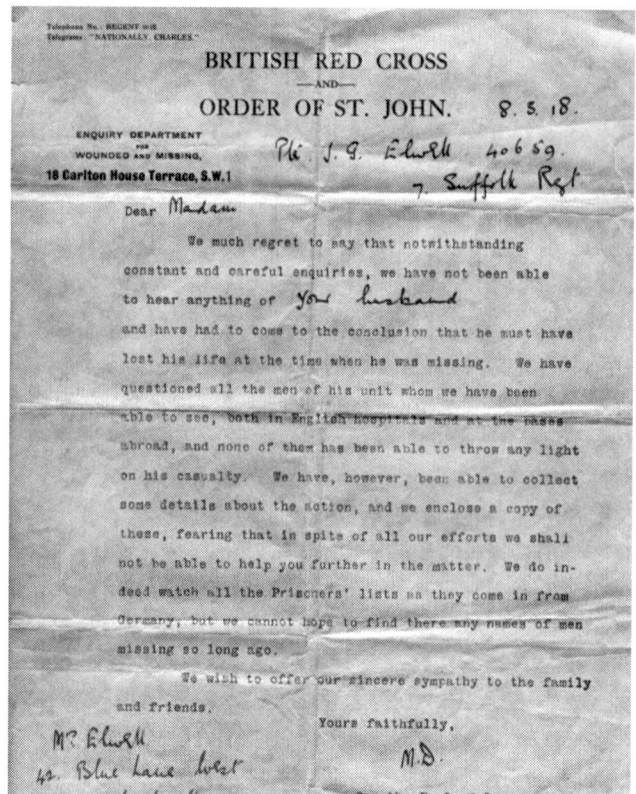

**Red Cross letter to Bertha, 8th March 1918 –
'...he must have lost his life.'**

'Your husband must have lost his life at the time he was (posted as) missing.'

So, almost eleven months after Jim had gone 'over the top' at Arras, officialdom had drawn the logical conclusion – or had it?

LETTER 70
[Wednesday, 14th March 1918. Written to Bertha by the Infantry Record Office, Warley.]

Six days later, the Infantry Record Office at Warley wrote to Bertha also expressing the opinion that Jim had been killed on 28th April 1917, the day he was officially posted as *'missing and wounded'*. However, the letter (see below) went on to add the proviso that:

'The term, "missing", does not necessarily mean that the soldier is killed or wounded. He may be an unwounded prisoner or temporarily separated from his regiment. Any further information will be at once sent to you.'

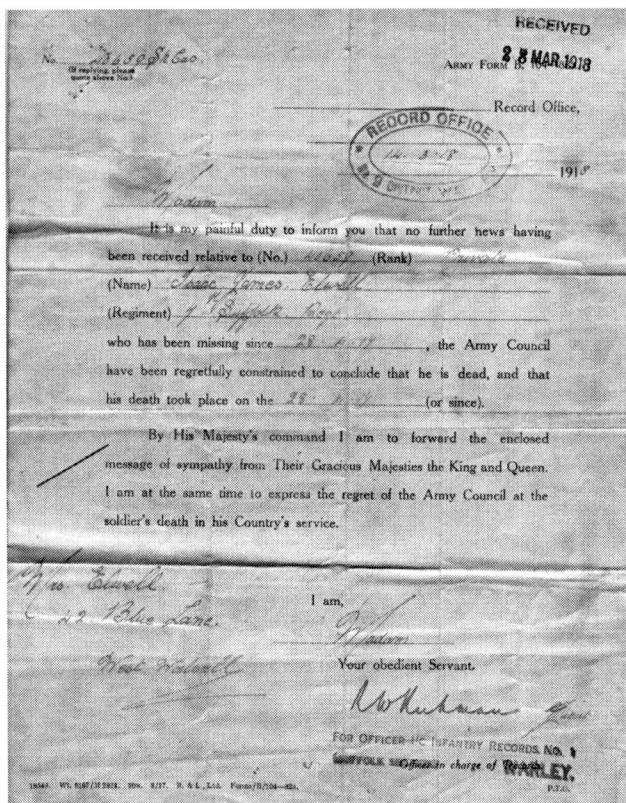

The third casualty letter, '...conclude that he is dead.'

Only a finely-tuned bureaucratic mind could state that a man had been killed but that he might not have been killed! If Bertha felt confused, it was entirely understandable and thus she continued to believe that Jim would eventually turn up.

(iii) A Glimmer of Hope

LETTER 71
[Thursday, 19 April 1918. Written by Mrs. E. Cantillion, 24, Southgate Street, Gloucester.]

Then came a bolt from the blue. A letter dated Thursday, 19th April 1918 from an Ethel Cantillion and postmarked *'Gloucester'* dropped through Bertha's letterbox; the woman was entirely unknown to Bertha but what she had to say caught her interest instantly:

'Dear madam, Just a line asking if your husband is in France as my husband is out there and he came across a few cards and a little girl's photo and I thought there would be no harm in writing as my husband thought you would like to have them back again. I have two little boys of my own and they try to write to their Dad but they are not old enough. But I think it was your two little girls that wrote to their dad. So. If you will please let me have an answer back I will forward them (to you).

Yours truly, Mrs. Cantillion.'

PS: 'If my husband ever picks up anything else he will forward it.'

One of the cards retrieved sometime later has survived; it is an embroidered card that reads, *'Birthday Greetings Across The Sea'* (see right), and on the obverse (on page 78) bears the poignant, hand-written message:

'Wishing dear Daddy Many Happy Returns, much love from Betty'.

Beneath the words from Jim's daughter Lizzie (signed as 'Betty'), and written in pencil, is the comment of Private Cantillion:

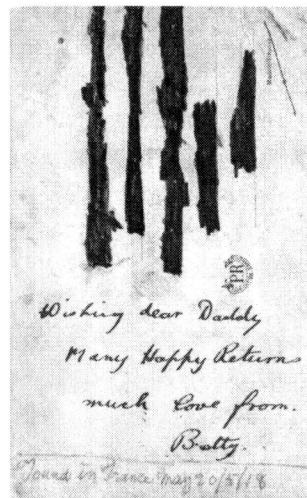

Lizzie (Betty's) message for Jim's 37th birthday, 3rd October 1916.

'Found in France May 20/5/18'.

Nowhere, in any of the subsequent letters between the two families, do Henry or Ethel Cantillion ever refer

Embroidered birthday card sent to Jim.

to the circumstances under which the cards and photo were found – it might have happened purely by chance but, given that the original discovery was apparently made during early 1918, it is quite probable that Private Cantillion was involved in 'clearing' the former Arras battlefield. If so, he would have come across numerous personal items of the fallen in what was a most harrowing task for even the most battle-hardened soldier. Whatever the origins of the find, the vital thing for Bertha was that the items would find their way home as her Walsall address appeared on at least one of the cards. The effect on Bertha of this unexpected revelation can scarcely be imagined – was it evidence Jim was still alive? Was it proof he had been killed? Yet again, her mind must have been in turmoil.

'In memoriam' notice in the 'Walsall Pioneer'
[Saturday, May 4, 1918.]

Despite the renewed hope stirred by the letter from Mrs. Ethel Cantillion, Bertha nevertheless decided to insert an 'In memoriam' notice in a local newspaper, the 'Walsall Pioneer', on Saturday, May 4, 1918. It read as follows:

> **Roll of Honour in Memoriam** 'In ever loving memory of my dear Husband, Private I.J. Elwell, of the 7th Suffolk Regiment, who was reported killed in action on April 28th, 1917; aged 37 years.
>
> You are not forgotten, husband dear,
> Nor will you ever be;
> As long as life and memory last
> We shall remember thee.
>
> Deeply mourned by his sorrowing Wife and children Lizzie and Lucy.'

LETTER 72
[Saturday, 25th May 1918. Written to Bertha by the Infantry Record Office, No.9 District, Warley.]

Bertha was obviously still torn between fearing the worst and hoping for the best but Ethel Cantillion's letter inspired Bertha to renew her enquiries at the Infantry Record Office. She probably reasoned that if some of Jim's personal effects had been found by Private Cantillion then others might have turned up elsewhere, so her letter was sent in late May of 1918. The reply was prompt but short and most discouraging:

> '....in reply to your enquiry of 23rd May 1918, no further articles of private property of the soldier have been received in this office.'

LETTER 73
[June 1918. Written to Bertha by the War Office, South Kensington, London.]

Within weeks another letter arrived, this time from London and this time from the War Office. Printed at the head of the letter was 'Effects Form 45G' and the content must have seemed chillingly final:

> '...the Command Paymaster…has been authorised to issue the sum of twelve shillings and ten pence being the amount that is due on the settlement of the accounts [that is, Jim's back pay] of the late No. 40659, Private Isaac James Elwell, 7th Battalion, Suffolk Regiment. Of the above amount, two thirds is the property of the deceased's children and must be used for their equal and exclusive benefit.
>
> I am, etc,
>
> C. Harris, Assistant Financial Secretary.'

There was no equivocation here – Jim was referred to as, '...the deceased'. After having her expectations raised by Ethel Cantillion's letter, Bertha had been dealt a heavy blow – yet she still refused to give up hope.

LETTER 74
[Undated, 1918. Written by Ethel Cantillion to Bertha.]

Bertha had evidently replied to Ethel Cantillion's initial letter and had offered to send her a photograph of Lizzie and Lucy. Ethel replied:

'I write in reply to your kind letter. I would be pleased to have your two little girls' photos and I will have ours taken this week and will send you one. I have a sister working up in Birmingham and I asked her if she would come to see you. I am expecting my husband home on leave next month and if he comes we will have a trip up there to see you. If my husband ever picks up anything else he will forward it.'

Ethel also attempted to offer Bertha renewed hope of finding Jim alive:

'I should not worry too much – there is a woman who had news that her husband had been killed a year ago and last Tuesday she had a letter to say he had been a prisoner with the Turks and that was the first letter they would allow him to write.'

Just as the letter from the War Office had severely dampened Bertha's waning optimism, so Ethel Cantillion's anecdote must have revived it. One may but imagine the continuing turmoil in her mind.

LETTER 75
[Undated, 1918. Written by Ethel Cantillion to Bertha.]

There then ensued a substantial break between letters. In her previous reply, Bertha had apparently sent a book for one of Ethel's children; she had also enquired whether Ethel's husband had seen anything of the crucifix from the rosary that Jim had carried with him everywhere [see letter 14 on pages 34-35 for details]. Ethel replied:

'....I have been away for five weeks.'
'I thank you very much from my eldest boy for the book.'
'My husband is alright – I wrote to tell him about the rosary – if you would like to write to him you could tell him better than I could.'
'This is my husband's address:-
292664, Pte H. J. Cantillion, 'B' Company, 3/10th Battalion, Middlesex Regiment, 'J' Infantry Base Depot, BEF, France.'

There is an apparent confusion here – the battalion given for Private Henry Cantillion's, 3/10th Middlesex, landed at Le Havre, France, on 1st June 1917 was

initially part of the South African Brigade, 9th 'Scottish' Division. Yet Private Cantillion was sent to France in April 1918 (see letter 79 on page 80) and thus must have been with another regiment prior to transfer to the Middlesex. 3/10th Middlesex subsequently transferred to 10th Brigade, 4th Division on 2nd August 1917 and was eventually disbanded on 20th February 1918 as a direct consequence of the reduction from four battalions to three per brigade in early 1918. Private Cantillion would have been posted to yet another battalion unless the Middlesex existed as a cadre[2].

LETTER 76
[Sunday, 23 June 1918. Written by Ethel Cantillion to Bertha.]

In Bertha's next letter to Ethel she had evidently suggested that the two families meet and, in the meantime, exchange photos. Ethel replied:

'It is very kind of you to mention staying a weekend. My husband thinks he will be having his leave and then we will have a trip up and see you. I should very much like one of your photos as I have had myself and my two little boys taken but they won't be done for another fortnight.'

This was to be the last letter from Gloucester for several weeks. Bertha must have been somewhat mystified.

LETTER 77
[July 1918. Written to Bertha by the Ministry of Pensions, Pensions Issue Office, Baker Street, London.]

In the heat of high summer, the post for once brought good news from the Ministry of Pensions:

'Under the terms of the recent Royal Warrant respecting pensions, you are entitled to a pension of 25/5 [£1.27p.] a week with effect from 1st May 1918. The new rate is made up as follows:- 13/9 [69p.] for yourself; 6/8 [33½p.] for your first child, 5/0 [25p.] for your second. Arrears amounting to 27/6 [£1.37½p.] .....will be paid.....by the Post Office on 17th July 1918.'

[2] A cadre was a 'skeleton' battalion that took no part in operations.

This increase in the pension rate, however small, would have been very welcome to Bertha who must have been struggling beneath a mountain of unspoken worry to make ends meet.

LETTER 78
[Friday, 28 August 1918. Written by Ethel Cantillion to Bertha.]

By late August, Bertha's photo of Lizzie and Lucy had arrived in Gloucester but the news that came back to Walsall was dreadful and explained the lack of letters from Ethel:

'I had bad news about three weeks ago....to say that my dear hubby was badly wounded[3] and was brought to Birmingham. When I heard again he had been transferred nearer (home) to Campden, about 9 miles from Gloucester. So I took my two little boys up to see him on Tuesday but I think he will be a cripple all his lifetime as he will have to wear a padded boot. When he gets a little better in walking then we will have a trip up to see you. It worries me to death whether he will have to have his leg off.'

Despite her mind-numbing worry, Ethel was still able to turn her thoughts to Bertha's family:

'What two dear little girls you have and what a lovely photo they make.

'I am very sorry to hear about you and your dear little children and I hope against hope that you will be much better by the time you get this letter.

'Yours sincerely, Ethel Cantillion (and) from Mike and from Stan.'
PS: This is my hubby's address if you would like to write to him:-

Pte. H.J. Cantillion, Norton Hall, Campden, Gloucestershire.'

Hearing such news must have sent all kinds of visions through Bertha's mind but now she became a friendly support for Ethel Cantillion and quickly decided to write to Ethel's husband.

LETTER 79
[Monday, 2 September 1918. Written by Pte. Henry Cantillion to Bertha. Headed – Norton Hall, Campden, Gloucestershire.]

Private Cantillion was evidently pleased to read Bertha's letter and replied promptly:

'Just a few lines in answer to your letter.

'My wife and children came to pay me a visit last Tuesday and it was quite a pleasure to see them after being out there for eighteen months…it is absolute murder out there; it is a pity - stop it as we are fighting for nothing, only causing misery in everybody back home.

'It must be terrible out there just at present now that we are advancing as I know what it is (like).'

The bitterness is clearly close to the surface – yet who could be surprised at the feelings of a man who had spent eighteen months on the Western Front? At this point it seemed that his leg was improving and that he might make a good recovery:

'My leg and foot are 'A1' again but still I don't want to go out there again.

'If we get the chance we will come up there to spend a couple of days with you. It must be hard for you without your husband.'

Bertha must have viewed a possible visit with somewhat mixed feelings.

LETTER 80
[Sunday, Undated, 1918. Written by Ethel Cantillion to Bertha.]

When he first returned wounded to 'Blighty', Henry Cantillion had been sent to hospital in Birmingham then, after a few weeks, had been transferred nearer home, to Norton Hall in Campden. It appears that while there he took a turn for the worse and had to be removed once again to Birmingham for treatment:

'My hubby is up in Birmingham now for a little while but I don't know how long he will be there. He told me they are keeping him in bed as they are putting his leg

---

[3] It is not possible to trace the action in which Private Henry Cantillion was wounded as the only battalion given for him, 3/10th Middlesex, was disbanded in February 1918 when brigade structure reduced the previous number of battalions from four to three. Along with all the other men whose battalions were disbanded, Private Cantillion would probably have been transferred to another battalion but no details have survived.

and foot in plaster of Paris which he said was like a hundredweight on his leg.

'I may come up to see you next month; don't be surprised to see him when he gets about – he would like to have a talk to you.

'I will have to close now as my two little boys are off to Sunday School – they are having their treat next week.

'This is my hubby's address:-

Private. H.J. Cantillion, 1st Southern General Hospital, Kings Heath Section, Ward B.5, Birmingham.'

Ironically, the hospital was but a few miles from Bertha's home in Walsall.

LETTER 81

[Wednesday 9 September 1918. Written by Ethel Cantillion to Bertha.]

By early September, the prognosis for Henry Cantillion's damaged leg was far from good:

'I am sorry I have not answered (your kind letter) but I have been worried over my hubby's leg as they thought he would have to have his leg off. From what the nurse said, they just escaped it as his foot and leg were quite green – I've never seen such a sight. It is wicked what the poor men have got to face in this wicked war. He has got to have a cripple boot made and padded all round the sides as his bones in his ankle are all smashed and he has a dreadful wound in his thumb.'

From the description, it seems that Private Cantillion was indeed fortunate not to lose his leg. At home in Gloucester, Ethel's two little lads were suffering from influenza – if it was the so-called 'Spanish Flu', then they were also fortunate to survive as the pandemic killed millions worldwide:

'I also have my two little boys in bed with this 'flu very bad but glad to say they are a little better.'

'I will send your two little girls a present in two or three days and hope to see you soon as soon as my hubby can get about.'

LETTER 82

[Undated, 1918. Part of a letter from Henry Cantillion to Bertha, headed – '1st Southern General Hospital, Kings Heath Section, Ward B.5, Birmingham.']

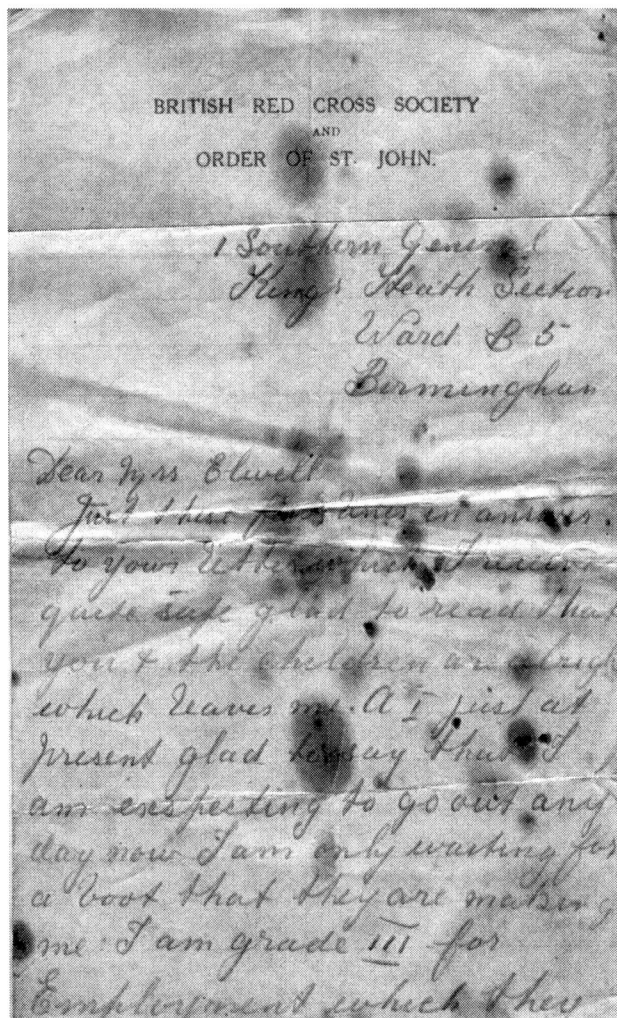

Letter to Bertha from Henry Cantillion in Kings Heath Hospital, Birmingham.

Bertha again took up Ethel Cantillion's invitation to write to her husband and the news he sent by return (above) was more encouraging:

'Just these few lines in answer to your letter. Glad to read that you and the children are alright. I am 'A1'. I'm expecting to go out any day now – I am only waiting for a boot that they are making for me. I am Grade III for employment.….'

According to the spoken evidence of Lucy, Jim Elwell's younger daughter, Henry Cantillion did in fact eventually visit Bertha and the girls in Walsall. What he said should have led Bertha to believe that Jim would *definitely* not be coming home – *how* he knew about it has not been recorded for posterity. Nevertheless, Bertha was undoubtedly very grateful to Henry Cantillion for returning the cards and photograph; yet, however overwhelming the evidence, she could never finally accept that Jim would not be coming home.

LETTER 83

[November 1918. Sent to Bertha by Walsall
War Pensions Committee.]

The final surviving letter to cross the Elwell threshold in November 1918 recorded a local mark of respect for Jim and furnished a short-term measure of financial support for the family. It came from the Walsall War Pensions Committee.

'This card must be produced each time that you call at this office.' [Payments of 5/0 (25p.) were paid to Bertha from 8/11/18 to 23/12/18 inclusive.]

Five shillings was not a great amount but everything helped at a time when Bertha was struggling to raise a young family on her own. Taken in conjunction with her war widow's pension, Bertha was briefly in receipt of thirty shillings and five pence per week – it was not exactly a fortune but it would help see the family through the winter of 1918-1919. Fortunately, a small amount of money was forthcoming from another source as Bertha had been able to take in a lodger, a soldier by the name of Joe Clifton [shown right]. Soon after the end of the Great War, Joe offered to marry Bertha but for many years she refused as she was always expecting a knock on the door to announce the return of her beloved Jim, whom she believed was suffering from amnesia.

Private Joe Clifton who asked Bertha to marry him soon after the end of the war.

CHAPTER NINE

Commemorations at home and abroad

After the Great War drew to a close, the authorities confirmed that, since Jim had neither turned up in France nor had come home as a repatriated prisoner of war, he had indeed been killed on the day that he was posted as missing – 28th April 1917. Bertha could never bring herself to accept the finality of this unwelcome decision and for years she retained in a corner of her heart the belief that, one day, Jim would appear at the front door.

Arras Memorial – cross and entrance archway.

In the meantime, cities, towns, villages and hamlets, businesses, councils, schools and churches, Walsall among them, were deciding how best to commemorate those who had lost their lives in the Great War. There was no standard form of local memorial or commemoration and Britain is the richer for the diversity, though nationally common threads are to be found.

At Whitehall in the heart of London the national Cenotaph was unveiled on 11th November 1920 by King George V, after which the king and his entourage slowly and solemnly walked behind the coffin that bore the body of the 'Unknown Soldier'[1] to Westminster Abbey. There the coffin passed through a guard of honour of one hundred holders of the Victoria Cross and was laid to rest at the west end of the nave. Six barrels of earth taken from Ypres lined the grave, that the soldier might lie on the soil where his compatriots

Arras Memorial – cemetery and cloisters.

had lost their lives. A military guard stood over the Tomb of the Unknown Soldier for seven days while countless thousands of mourners filed past to pay their respects to fathers, sons, husbands and brothers who had fallen in the war, the missing and the identified alike. A week later the grave was sealed with a stone inscribed with the words:-

'A British Warrior Who Fell in the Great War
1914-1918 for King and Country. Greater Love
Hath No Man Than This.'

Campaign medals were awarded to those who had served during the Great War. Those who came under fire in 1914 or 1915 were awarded either the 1914 'Mons' Star (for service up to 22nd November 1914) or the 1914-1915 Star (for service from 23rd November 1914 to 31st December 1915). In recognition of service abroad, men were

Jim's British War Medal (left) and Victory Medal.

[1] The bodies of four unidentified soldiers were exhumed from cemeteries in Ypres, Arras, the Somme and the Aisne and taken to St. Pol in northern France where one was chosen at random to be the 'Unknown Soldier'. The other three were re-interred in a nearby cemetery.

Memorial Plaque sent to Bertha after the war. This was also known as a 'Dead Man's Penny.'

awarded the silver British War Medal and the bronze-lacquered Victory Medal – Jim Elwell was entitled to both of the latter two (see Jim's two medals on page 83).

Jim's family, like the family of each serviceman killed in the war, was presented with a Bronze Memorial Plaque[2], several inches across and engraved with Jim Elwell's name (above). A Memorial Scroll from King George V, thanking the family for their sacrifice, accompanied the plaque that was known colloquially and harshly as the 'Dead Man's Penny'.

After the armistice, all along the old battlefronts and near to the former Casualty Clearing Stations and Stationary and Base Hospitals, temporary cemeteries were tidied and formalised, while small battlefield burials were recovered and concentrated in larger cemeteries. Charged with the massive responsibility of organising the final resting places of several hundred thousand servicemen was the Imperial (later renamed Commonwealth) War Graves Commission. In time, the original wooden battlefield crosses were replaced by commission-produced standard headstones, usually of limestone, and inscribed with a man's military details; if they so wished, a family might add a few words of their own[3]. These cemeteries, some containing several thousands of graves, have been immaculately maintained by the unsung gardeners of the Commission for almost a century and, ironically, are among the most peaceful and beautiful of places. Yet this did not address the plight of the men who had been reported as 'missing'; as there was no body to bury, how were they to be commemorated? The adopted solution was to raise monumental 'Memorials to the Missing' at key locations along the old Western Front, in all other theatres of war and on naval memorials at Chatham, Plymouth and Portsmouth. On each memorial, the

Arras Memorial, Suffolk Regiment panel.

[2] Known colloquially as the 'Dead Man's Penny'.
[3] In Britain, families were expected to pay for this privilege; present-day Commonwealth countries refused to pay for what they viewed as a family's right.

Arras Memorial, Jim Elwell's name on the Suffolk
Regiment panel.

OUR VALIANT DEAD.

SCROLL OF HONOUR.

Of those who have made the supreme sacrifice in the R.C. Parish of
St. Patrick's, Blue Lane, Walsall.

¶ *"Greater love than this no man hath, that a man lay down his life for his friends."*

Thomas Fallon	Thomas Kennedy	Thomas Cooper
Thomas Elton	George Ryan	Alfred Hodson
Michael Elton	Richard Wollaston	Michael Gallagher
Peter Degville	J. Bowen	John Ward
A.S. Francis Cooley	William Marshall	William Higgins
Peter Coyne	Benjamin Swinnerton	James Elwell
Joseph Yates	Thomas Dinsdale	Thomas Burns
Sgt. William Purley	William Thorpe	James Dolan
Luke Kennedy	Harry Keele	Henry Snell
A.S. Walter James	Harry Kelly	Patrick Nolan
Harry Kelly	Patrick Moylan	Peter Donlon
Sgt. Frank Wollaston	James Roach	George Downing
John Ledwidge	Frank Maley	Kevin Cuthbert Moran
L/Cpl. George Pitt	John Dunlavey	Wilfred Saunders
Andrew James	Patrick Walshe	Edward Maley
Thomas Sheedy	Alfred Hawkeswood	Edward Egan
Thomas Murphy	George Jones	Michael Blewitt
Frank Lycett	Coy. Sgt.-Mjr. W. H. Rickards	Thomas Blewitt
John Chas. Horden	John McCormack	Fred Walters
A.S. Chad Wilde	George Adams	John Johnson
A.S. Thomas Bird	William Higgs	Bernard John Connolly
John Donlan	William McNally	Michael McNally
Sgt.-Mjr. Dahamel	Edward Killala	Ed. Yates
John Francis Price	Ldg. Signalman John Snell	Sydney Moran
William Hardman	George Somerfield	Charles Smith
2nd-Lieut. E. P. Underwood	Thomas Reddy	George Hart
Bernard Jones	John Russell	Ed. Dumphy, M. M.
Martin Burns	Chas. Fisher	Edward Mullins
Fred Burton	William Hannon	L/Cpl. George Henry Littler
Alfred Dunphy	Owen McDonald	John Higgins
Cpl. John Kane	Michael Doyle	Cpl. Joseph Navin
James Hughes	Sgt. John Kelly, D.C.M.	P.O. Joseph Cunningham
L/Cpl. John Stringer	Joseph Neary	Sgt. John Rudge
William Wood	Cadet John Henry Hale	Thomas Bland
Sgt. John Mannion	Cpl. John Donelly	Sgt.-Mjr. Thomas Hawkeswood
Michael Higgins	Sgt. Edward Maley	Patrick Welch
Cpl. John McNally	Sidney Smith	John Ward
L/Cpl. James Farrell	Thomas McDonald	Bernard Porter
Patrick McDonald	John Cunningham	John Doyle
James Webster	L/Cpl. William Watkins	Thomas Glennon
John Hogan	Sydney Joseph Powell	Arthur Bernard Miller
Thomas Murphy		

¶ *"In the sight of the unwise they seemed to die; and their departure was taken for misery: and their going away from us, for utter destruction: but they are in peace."*

Henry McDonell

St. Patrick's R.C. Church Roll of Honour, 1914-1919.

panels are usually organised in order of regimental seniority and by rank and many bear a dedication similar to the one adorning the Menin Gate Memorial to the Missing:

'Here are recorded the names of officers and men who fell in the Ypres Salient but to whom the fortune of war denied the known and honoured burial given to their comrades in death.'

On the Arras Memorial to the Missing are recorded the names of 35,942 officers and men who fell in the Arras sector and whose bodies were never identified. Jim Elwell's name is duly inscribed on the Suffolk Regiment panel (see page 84) in bay 4 of the memorial that stands in the Faubourg-d'Amiens Cemetery on the Boulevard du General de Gaulle in the western part of the town of Arras (see page 83). The memorial was designed by Sir Edwin Lutyens, the designer of the Cenotaph, and is in a beautifully peaceful setting. Jim is thus appropriately commemorated in a city where he spent so much of his war service with 7th Suffolk and 69th Field Company, Royal Engineers.

At Feuchy Chapelle, on the Arras-Cambrai road and just south of the start line for Jim's battalion on 28th April (see map 3 on page 69), is to be found a memorial to the 12th 'Eastern' Division, Jim's division. The stone cross, a copy of one in York Minster, is on the site of a dugout that once housed the old divisional head-quarters and is one of two memorials to the 12th Division on the Western Front. The other 12th Division memorial is to be found to the south of Cambrai, at Malassise Farm, near Epehy, and commemorates battles fought by the division during the eighteen months after Jim Elwell's sad demise.

Closer to home, in 1919, Walsall Corporation produced a book of commemoration in honour of its citizens. It explained the role of Walsall and its people during the war, offered a provisional town roll of honour, gave details of all the town's memorial services and included individual rolls of honour for schools, businesses, churches and other organisations. Within the book, which is entitled, *'Borough of Walsall Official Programme of Peace Celebrations & War Memorial, 1919'*, Jim's name is among more than 120 men commemorated on the St. Patrick's Church Scroll of Honour that is signed by Father MacDonell (above); here, Jim's name is given as 'James Elwell', rather than 'Isaac James Elwell'. Nevertheless, Jim would have been pleased that he was remembered at the church that had meant so much to him during his lifetime. His name, again written as, 'J. Elwell', also appears on page xxxv, of the main 'Walsall Roll of Honour'. A copy of the *'Peace Celebrations, 1919'* book is to be found on the shelves of the Walsall History Centre in Essex Street.

On 24th July 1919 a decision was taken by the local Council on the form of a more enduring Walsall War Memorial – a Cenotaph was to be raised in Bradford Street, bronze tablets (see page 86, top)) inscribed with the names of the fallen were to adorn the inside walls of the Town Hall, a roll of honour was to be scribed on vellum and four memorial playing fields were to be appropriately dedicated. On Saturday, 1st October 1921, the Cenotaph was unveiled; it bears the inscription:

Memorial tablet, Walsall Town Hall; Jim Elwell's name appears in the column second from the right.

'To the glory of God and in love and gratitude to the men of this borough who gave their lives for their country in the great world war of 1914-1918, this Cenotaph has been erected. Their name liveth for evermore.'   1st October 1921

'They were numbered among those who, at the call of King and Country, left all that was dear to them, endured hardness, faced danger and finally passed out of sight of men by the path of duty and self-sacrifice, giving up their own lives that others might live in freedom. Let those that come after see to it that their names be not forgotten.'

The interior of the Walsall Town Hall itself is in effect a huge war memorial. Ranged along both side walls are:

'...handsome bronze tablets, each surmounted by the borough coat of arms...all are beautifully lettered in cream enamel [with the names of the 1,992 Walsall men killed] and the principal tablet bears the inscription:-

"To the glory of God and in love and gratitude to the men of this borough who gave their lives for their country in the great world war of 1914-1918, this Cenotaph has been erected. Their name liveth for evermore."'

Jim Elwell is commemorated on the very first bronze plaque to the left of the front entrance, though for some unknown reason he is recorded as 'J.G. Elwell' (top right). Jim's name is also recorded in two beautiful volumes that were prepared under the supervision of

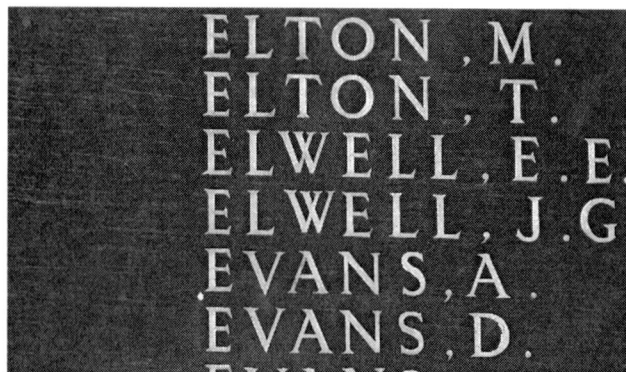

Town Hall memorial plaque.

Mr. R.R. Carter, the headmaster of the School of Art. The previous year, on 21st February 1920, and set at either side of the stage and its tiered seating, were unveiled two frescoes depicting the local battalion, 1/5th South Staffordshire, involved in their two most memorable actions, the Assault on the Hohenzollern Redoubt at Loos on 13th October 1915 and the Breaking of the Hindenburg Line on 29th September 1918 (one of the world's greatest feats of arms). The frescoes were painted and presented by Frank O. Salisbury.

Staffordshire Roll of Honour on display in Lichfield Cathedral.

Some time during the years immediately following the armistice, a large, beautifully scribed and heavily bound book (above) was produced, recording the names of most of the men of Staffordshire who died in the service of their country. It was organised alphabetically by town and village, giving a man's name, rank and regiment. This superb tome is on display in the South Staffordshire Regiment's chapel in Lichfield Cathedral, while simply-produced printed copies (published in 1926) are available for perusal in the cathedral and in the Walsall Local History Centre[4]. Jim Elwell's name is again recorded as, 'J.G. Elwell, Private,

[4] The centre is to be found in Essex Street, Walsall.

Suffolk Regiment.' This mistake probably replicates the mistake on the tablet in Walsall Town Hall.

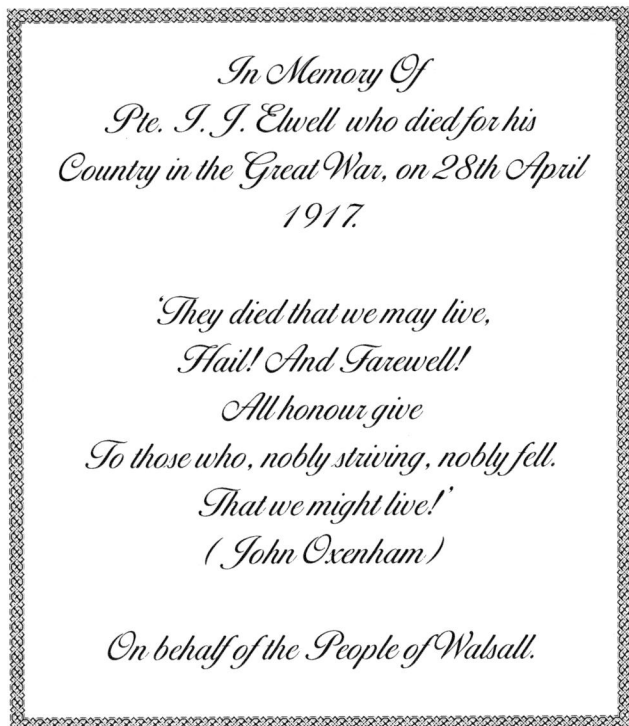

In Memory Of
Pte. I. J. Elwell who died for his
Country in the Great War, on 28th April
1917.

'They died that we may live,
Hail! And Farewell!
All honour give
To those who, nobly striving, nobly fell.
That we might live!'
(John Oxenham)

On behalf of the People of Walsall.

Another local act of memorial was instigated by Walsall Corporation with the issuing of a local scroll in recognition of the services rendered by the war dead of the town, thus Jim's family received a commemorative scroll, a transcription of which is shown above.

During the years immediately following the war the names of all soldiers killed in the conflict were catalogued by regiment, in a huge undertaking finally published in 1921, known as 'Soldiers and Officers Died in the Great War'. This gave rise to a work of eighty-one volumes and was not only a fitting memorial to those who died but also an excellent research tool listing more than 655,000 men and more than 37,000 officers. In 1998, this great work was transferred to CD-Rom, making access to the records easier. Jim Elwell appears under 7th Battalion, the Suffolk Regiment, his entry reading:-

40659 Private Isaac James Elwell; 7th Battalion, the Suffolk
Regiment;
Born in Birmingham; Enlisted in Walsall;
Killed in action in France & Flanders on 28/4/17.

Taken as a whole, the commemorations of Jim Elwell's life and death do justice to a family man who went off determined to 'do his bit' and to make the best of near impossible circumstances. Like so many other 'civilian' soldiers of 1914-1918, the worker in a saddlery hardware store went to learn a trade of which he knew

nothing and probably wanted to know even less. All he really wanted was to carve a comfortable life with Bertha and to bring up their two young girls, Lizzie and Lucy, as best they possibly could. It was not to be. Let Jim's own words have the final say:

'The people in England don't know there's a war on especially young men that are fit and well enough to fight or they would be out here helping to fight or doing some little bit towards bringing to a close this cruel war. Thank God I am trying to do my little bit in it, live or die.'

40659 Private I.J. Elwell, letter home on 28th October 1916, written while in reserve line billets in the shell-torn city of Arras.

HE whom this scroll commemorates was numbered among those who, at the call of King and Country, left all that was dear to them, endured hardness, faced danger, and finally passed out of the sight of men by the path of duty and self-sacrifice, giving up their own lives that others might live in freedom. Let those who come after see to it that his name be not forgotten.

40659, PRIVATE, Isaac James ELWELL

7th Battalion.
Suffolk Regiment
Killed in action, France & Flanders, 28/04/17
Born: Birmingham, Enlisted: Walsall,
FORMERLY 2607, S. STAFFS. REGT.

Royal scroll of condolence sent to Bertha after the war.

CHAPTER TEN

Epilogue

On 29th April 1917, the day after Jim was killed, his battalion, 7th Suffolk, was withdrawn from the front line but this was by no means the end of their participation in the Battles of Arras. Just four days later, on 3rd and 4th May, the battalion was committed to the Third Battle of the Scarpe and on 12th May it made its final major assault in the sector during the attack on Devil's Trench. Six months passed before 7th Suffolk played another leading role, this time in the Battle of Cambrai, being involved in all three of the actions between 20th November and 3rd December – as a result, by the end of 1917 the battalion had lost another 175 men killed and hundreds more wounded. The late winter of 1917-1918 was relatively quiet but only because the German High Command was planning the last-ditch, massive, '*Kaiserschlacht*' spring offensive that was designed to break the British and French lines and force an armistice before the newly-arrived American troops could swing the balance in the Allies' favour. The Suffolks found themselves in the Somme sector where the storm broke and they fought desperately in the Battle of Bapaume (25th March 1918) before being driven back to Arras where they again stood and fought on 28th March. A week later, on 5th April, they were fighting on the River Ancre as the British were pushed further and further backwards; this retreat continued until finally, almost at breaking point, the line held outside Amiens – a distance of forty miles from the site of the opening assault. The Ancre proved to be the swansong of 7th Suffolk as, having lost 119 men killed since the '*Kaiserschlacht*' broke on 21st March, the battalion was broken up on 19th May 1918, though the surviving eleven officers and 404 other ranks were transferred to 1/1st Battalion, the Cambridgeshire Regiment. The old battalion had finally gone the way of so many of the soldiers that had served in it.

On the home front Bertha, still convinced that Jim would one day return, continued to live in Walsall and eventually, more than twenty years after reading that fateful letter telling her Jim had been '*…slightly wounded*', she agreed to marry Joe Clifton, a good man who had been so kind to the family in the difficult years after the Great War. Her long, painful vigil was over.

In the months that followed the end of the Great War, an unusual offer had come Bertha's way from the Gloucester family that had befriended the Elwells in the wake of Jim's death. Mr. Cantillion wanted to adopt Lucy after the war as he and his wife, Ethel, had no girls and they thought it would serve to make life easier for Bertha. As is now evident, Lucy remained with Bertha and Lizzie, eventually marrying Fred Cooper and having three daughters of her own, twins Iris and Marie in 1938 and Christine in 1944. Lucy, the longest surviving direct link with Jim, sadly died in March 2008 at the age of ninety-seven. Lizzie, known to most of the family as Hilda, married Fred Haywood and they too had daughters, Brenda and Maureen.

Jim's younger brother, Ted, survived the war and he and Nell, Bertha's sister, had a son, also named Ted.

Jim Powell's grandson, Fred Powell (see page 90) remembers his great-aunt Bertha, '*…always seeming to have jars of sweets under the chaise long and she often shared the sweets with the children next door at number 41.*'

Bertha was to suffer yet another heartache on 17th March 1951 when Joe Clifton died at the age of 71. She was to survive him by just two years. After what had never been an easy life, Bertha died on 18th July 1953 and is buried in plot 50.2.200 of Ryecroft Cemetery, Walsall – reunited with Joe and, at long, long last, with her beloved Jim whose name is inscribed at the top of Bertha's headstone (below).

Reunited.

APPENDIX ONE

The units in which Jim Elwell served, June 1916 – April 1917

June 1916 – Called up for military service. Joined 16 Platoon (later 13 Platoon), 'D' Company, 1/6th **South Staffordshire Regiment** then 'D' Company, 1/5th Battalion, South Staffordshire Regiment Training Reserve, Scotton Camp, Catterick, Yorkshire, England.

Between 20th and 27th September 1916 – Left Scotton and crossed the Channel to France. Joined 1/6th Battalion, the **South Staffordshire Regiment**, 137th 'Staffordshire' Brigade, 46th '1st North Midland' Division. Bailleulmont/Berles-au-Bois sector, Northern Somme, France.

Soon after 10th October 1916 – Followed a number of Walsall men on transfer to 14 Platoon, 'D' Company, 7th Battalion, the **Suffolk Regiment**, 35th Brigade, 12th 'Eastern' Division. Near Bernafay Wood, Somme sector, France. Battalion moved to the Arras sector of the front on 22nd October where it remained until late into 1917.

Probably 19th or 20th March 1917 – Attached temporarily to 69th Field Company, **Royal Engineers**, 12th 'Eastern' Division. Remained in the same general area near Arras, France.

Probably 11th April 1917 – Returned to 'D' Company, **7th Suffolk**. In the Feuchy Chapelle sector, to the southeast of Arras.

28th April 1917 – Initially wounded in action with 7th Suffolk on Orange Hill at the Battle of Arleux and presumed then to have been killed by enemy action while being moved down the line to a casualty clearing station. Many months later was assumed to have died on 28th April 1917.

Notes on Jim's units, 1916/1917:

1/6th Battalion, the South Staffordshire Regiment was one of four battalions in 137th 'Staffordshire' Brigade – the other three were 1/5th South Staffordshire, 1/5th North Staffordshire and 1/6th North Staffordshire. 137th Brigade, along with 138th 'Lincolnshire and Leicestershire' Brigade and 139th 'Sherwood Foresters' Brigade constituted the 46th 'North Midland' Division, the first complete Territorial Division to serve on the Western Front, landing in France on 3rd March 1915. As a Walsall lad, in the early years war Jim would have expected to serve in the local battalion, 1/5th South Staffordshire, but by 1916 men were directed to the battalion in greatest need of replacements, thus Jim went to 1/6th South Staffordshire, a battalion that was raised in Wolverhampton rather than Walsall. However, it transpired that 12th 'Eastern' Division had even greater need of men and Jim was soon transferred to 7th Suffolk.

7th Battalion, the Suffolk Regiment was one of four battalions in 35th Brigade – the other three were 7th Norfolk, 9th Essex and 5th Royal Berkshire. 35th Brigade, along with 36th and 37th Brigades constituted the 12th 'Eastern' Division. This division was one of the first 'New Army' units to be formed and landed in France between 1st and 5th June 1915. By the time of Jim Elwell's transfer to 7th Suffolk, it had become an experienced battalion, having fought in the Battle of Loos in 1915 and on the Somme in 1916. While Jim was with the battalion it fought again on the Somme in 1916 and at Arras in 1917.

69th Field Company was one of the three companies of Royal Engineers that served as part of 12th 'Eastern' Division – the others were 70th Field Company and 87th Field Company. Their duties were wide-ranging and included bridge-building, road and railway building, all aspects of entrenching – in short, anything that required specialist construction (or, for that matter, destruction) skills. The 69th served with 12th Division throughout the Great War and played a pivotal role in the complex preparations for the opening of the Arras campaign of 9th April 1917.

APPENDIX TWO

Family, friends, workmates and soldiers mentioned in the letters

Jim's family members mentioned in the letters:

Jim's nan:	Elizabeth Elwell.
Parents:	Joe and Martha Elwell (née Wassall).
Wife:	Bertha (daughter of William and Sarah Webster) who had eight sisters and one brother, including MaryAnn Webster (who married Jim Powell), Maria Webster (who married Sidney Powell), Sophia Wynifred Webster (who married Fred Swain) and Henry Webster (who married Alice Powell).
Children:	Lizzie (Elizabeth Hilda) and Lucy Marie ('the little'uns').
Sisters:	Martha – married Joe Boddice. Elizabeth (known as Lizzie). MaryAnn (known as Polly) – married Theo Neville. Rosetta (known as Rose) – married Tom Spencer, who also served in the army. Lucy – married a reputedly wealthy man, Harry North, went to live in Birmingham and was never seen again by the family. Ellen, (known as Nell) – married Will Simpson, who also served in the army.
Brothers:	Joseph Henry – drowned, 8th August 1880, aged nine. Joseph Edward (known as Ted) – married Bertha's sister, Nell Webster (Nell died, aged 89, on 7th December 1981). Ted served in the army, joining up before Jim and maybe wounded; possibly sometime as 'Signaller J. or T. Elwell, No.20955, No. 1 Coy, 16th Cheshire, Chester Castle, Chester.' Ted and Nell had a son, Edward, who still lives in Ryecroft.

Harry Wassall:	Cousin on Jim's mother's side (Martha Wassall). Killed in action on 2nd July 1916 [see the obituary on page 92].

Bertha's mother:	Sarah Hawkins who married William Webster.

Fred and Sophia Swain (née Webster):	Sophia was Bertha's sister and often known by her second name, Wynifred.

Alice Powell:	Born in 1878. Married Henry Webster and lived in Blue Lane.

Fred and Teresa Powell (née Moore):	Alice's older brother, Fred was born in 1872 and he owned numbers 41 and 42, Blue Lane West and thus was Jim and Bertha's landlord and next-door neighbour. Fred Powell bought the two houses around 1900 for good reasons – though built in about 1820, they were high quality and possessed hot and cold running water; crucially, at the rear of the houses was a large stable that was ideal for converting into a small brass and nickel foundry that would later produce all the trappings of the loriner's craft.

Jim and MaryAnn Powell (née Webster, Bertha's sister):	Fred's younger brother, Jim was born in 1888; MaryAnn was one of Bertha's sisters. The couple lived in Newlands Street, Leamore and Jim worked at Broadhurst's. Jim and MaryAnn's daughter, Teresa, was mentioned in one of Jim Elwell's letters; a photo of mother and daughter is shown on page 33. Jim and MaryAnn's other child was James (see 'Jim and Maud' below). Jim Powell died of Spanish 'flu in 1918.

Jim and Maud Powell (née Wood):	Jim was the son of Jim and MaryAnn (above); he and Maud moved into number 41, Blue Lane West in 1935, most convenient for Jim's work in the small metal foundry at the back of the house. Jim began work at the foundry in 1927, aged fourteen, and was well taught by his Uncle Fred. In the

Fred Powell (Jr.).

APPENDICES

1930's Jim experimented with a nickel alloy so successfully that his Uncle Fred won the contract to make all the deck-rail fittings for the luxury liners, 'Queen Mary' and 'Queen Elizabeth', a task that took a year to complete. Moreover, Jim made the horse furniture for the horses that pulled the Coronation Coach in 1953. Jim and Maud had four children, the youngest of whom, young Fred (see page 90), worked the foundry from 1957 producing, among many other things, jack-spurs for the Royal Canadian Mounted Police. During the 1960's Fred moved the business to Shaws Street, Walsall where he made brass castings such as horse brasses, hames for the horses and brass figures. Fred later supervised the removal to and rebuild of the entire Shaws Street foundry at the Black Country Museum in Dudley, where he subsequently worked for years as a demonstrator. Although Fred has been left some time, he occasionally returns to the BCM for special events such as the heavy horse weekend, bonfire night and Christmas carol evenings. Fred also produced the sketch of the houses in Blue Lane West where the Elwells and the Powells lived.

Sid and Maria Powell (née Webster, Bertha's sister): Lived at 29, Newlands Street, close by Jim and MaryAnn. Sid worked as an iron-caster, as did all his sons. They had a large family, though several died as infants or as young children (at least three were named 'Siddy'); all of the children were musically gifted. The two children mentioned by name in Jim's letters were – 'young' Sid (Siddy) Powell, who was killed in Belgium in late 1917 [see the obituary below] and Bertha Powell, a daughter born during 1917.

Arthur Dix: Married Phoebe Boddice, daughter of Martha and Joe Boddice. Arthur and Phoebe later emigrated to Salt Lake City, Utah and converted to Mormonism. Phoebe died in 1983.

Friends and workmates mentioned in the letters:

Mr. Jagger: Albert Jagger – Jim's employer.
S.B. Jagger: Employer (son of Albert Jagger).
Freddie Wood: Workmate at SBJ.
Bailey, Marson and Mr. Stanley: Workmates at SBJ.
Mr. Case: Known through work.
Charlie Neville: Probably related to the husband of Jim's sister Polly.
Ada Peabody: Known through work.
Emmie: Known through work.
Little Ida: Known through Bertha's workplace.
Jack Jurdy [spelling uncertain], Florry Russell and Annie: Known through Bertha's workplace.
Mrs. P. Partridge: Neighbour who often looked after Jim's children.
Friends at Day Street: Connection unknown.
Mr. Stringer's son: Connection unknown.
Mrs. Hickson: Connection unknown.

Men from St. Patrick's Roman Catholic Church, Blue Lane West

Father Roskell: married Jim and Bertha in September 1908.
Father McDonell.
Father Clavin.
'Young' Smith: Reference unknown.
Edward Killala: Killed in action [see the obituary on page 92].

Soldiers mentioned in Jim Elwell's letters:

Edward 'Ted' ELWELL see page 90 for details.

GIBBS Private, 7th (Service) Battalion, the **Suffolk Regiment** (35th Brigade, 12th 'Eastern' Division). [No further information is available.]

'Young' JOE Private, 1/6th (Territorial Force) Battalion, the **South Staffordshire Regiment**. [No further information is available.]

George JONES Born in Walsall. Son of Ellen and the late William Henry Jones of Walsall. Lived at 104, Wolverhampton Street, Walsall. Employed in the Birmingham Canal Toll Office, West Bromwich. Single. Enlisted in 1915 in Walsall. Private, 40199, 7th (Service) Battalion, the **South Staffordshire Regiment** (33rd Brigade, 11th 'Northern' Division). *Unit History* – Landed in France in mid-September 1916. *Somme*, 15-22/9/16 Battle of Flers-Courcelette; 26-28/9/16 Battle of Thiepval. In action in Hessian and Zollern Trenches at end of September. Out of the line from 1st October. *Died from the effects of poison gas on 29/11/16 (aged 20) a few hours after admission to either 9th or 49th CCS.* Buried in plot VII. A. 33 of **Contay British Cemetery**, Contay, Somme, France. The family inscription on his headstone reads, *'Into thy hands I commend my spirit. Thou hast redeemed me O Lord'*. Report appears in the 23rd December 1916 edition of the *'Walsall Observer'*. [Photograph of headstone on page 51].

Edward KILLALA Born in Walsall. Lived at 4, Moat Road, Walsall. Educated at St. Mary's RC School. Single. Employed as a cutter by J. Shannon and Sons Ltd. Enlisted in Walsall. Private, 43292, 10th (Service) Battalion, the **Sherwood Foresters Regiment** (51st Brigade, 17th 'Northern' Division). *Unit History –* Landed in France on 14th December 1916. No major engagements. *Killed in action on Friday, 4/2/17 (aged 20)* in the Ancre sector. Commemorated on pier and face 10C of the **Thiepval Memorial to the Missing**, Somme, France. Two brothers served, one was in hospital in March 1917 and the other served at Salonika. Report appears in the 10th March 1917 edition of the *'Walsall Observer'*. [Photograph of panel from the Thiepval Memorial on page 62].

Sidney Joseph POWELL Born in Walsall. Son of Sidney John and Maria Powell of 29, Newlands Street, Walsall. Enlisted in Walsall. Private, 203585, 1st(Regular) Battalion, the **Lincolnshire Regiment** (62nd Brigade, 21st Division). *Unit History –* Arras 20/5-16/6/17 Actions on the Hindenburg Line. *3rd Ypres* (Passchendaele) 26/9-3/10/17 Battle of Polygon Wood; 4/10/17 Battle of Broodseinde. *Died on 6/10/17 (aged19) of wounds sustained* attacking Judge Copse in the Battle of Broodseinde during 3rd Ypres. Buried in plot XX. G. 5A of **Lijssenthoek Military Cemetery**, west of Ypres, Belgium. [Photograph of headstone on page 63].

Frank TOWNROW Born in Chesterfield, Derbyshire. Lived at 72, Whitehouse Street, Walsall. Stocktaker employed at the Birmingham branch of Butler's Springfield Brewery, Wolverhampton. Married. Enlisted in June 1916 in Birmingham. Private, 40637, 7th (Service) Battalion, the **Suffolk Regiment** (35th Brigade, 12th 'Eastern' Division) and formerly 2599, the South Staffordshire Regiment. *Unit History –* arrived in France on 16th September 1916 and transferred to 7/Suffolk; no major engagements. *Died of severe wounds to both legs on Tuesday, 15/3/17 (aged 39).* Buried in plot V. L. 4 of **Habarcq Communal Cemetery Extension**, Pas de Calais, France (west of Arras). Left a widow, Ellen, and five children. Three brothers served, Ernest and Roland in the army and William in the Royal Flying Corps. Report in the 31st March 1917 edition of the *'Walsall Observer'*. [Photograph of headstone on page 60].

Harry WASSALL Born in Birmingham. Enlisted in Birmingham. Private, 1843, 2/5th (Territorial Force) Battalion, the **Royal Warwickshire Regiment** (182nd Brigade, 61st '2nd South Midland' Division). *Unit History –* 21/5/16 landed in France. *Killed in action on Sunday, 2/7/16.* Buried in plot I. H. 2 of **Rue du Bacquerot No.1 Military Cemetery**, Laventie, Pas de Calais, France. [Wassall was the maiden name of Jim Elwell's mother, Martha, thus he was Jim's cousin.] [Photograph of headstone on page 40].

Alfred 'Johnny' WALKER Private, 7th (Service) Battalion, the **Suffolk Regiment** (35th Brigade, 12th 'Eastern' Division) and formerly 1/6th (Territorial Force) Battalion, the South Staffordshire Regiment. Served from June 1916, wounded at least once and survived the war. Bertha's cousin.

British soldiers, '…somewhere in France.'

APPENDIX THREE
The Elwell Papers

(i) The Letters

The Elwell Papers, now in the possession of Jim's great-granddaughter, Elaine Cox, comprise a substantial number of letters, photographs and sundry other items. Their common theme is a direct connection to Jim Elwell and, as such, furnish a remarkable insight into the life of an ordinary lad caught up in the horrors of the Great War; what is more, the official correspondence that was generated by Jim being posted as 'missing in action' opens a window on the struggles of the family he left behind – common enough after the war but infrequently so well documented.

Of the eighty-three surviving letters and cards, fifty-two were written and sent by Jim either from training camps in England (June to September 1916) or from various locations on the Western Front in northern France (September 1916 to April 1917). Jim's writings consist of a large number of pencil-written letters, sometimes on headed or decorated notepaper, sometimes on pages torn from a notebook – whatever he could find at the time; there are several picture postcards written whilst training in England and a few Field Service Postcards with their *'delete as appropriate'* instructions (these include Jim's last ever communication from France). All but one of his letters and cards were addressed to Bertha and the girls (and on two occasions to 'Granny' as well) – the exception was sent to Jim's mother and father.

Four of the letters written by Bertha to Jim have survived, simply because they arrived at his unit after Jim had been posted 'missing'; the letters, complete with their envelopes – one, clearly postmarked 'WALSALL, 6 PM, 18 AP 17', still bears the handwritten comment in pencil, *'wounded'* and is officially stamped *'present location uncertain'*. None of Bertha's letters that reached Jim have survived because as he put it, *'I destroy them…after I have read them because I have nowhere to keep them,'* – understandable sentiments in a wet, muddy trench in the depths of one of the worst winters in living memory. There is one other surviving letter written by Bertha to an official organisation; addressed to the Infantry Record Office at Warley, it was a plea for more information following notification that Jim had been wounded in action.

The balance of twenty-six letters comprise nine from Henry and Ethel Cantillion, a letter from Bertha's cousin, Alf Walker, a letter from a Liberal Party parliamentary candidate, seven official letters in respect of Jim's casualty status and finally eight official letters relating to wartime Separation Allowance and later Army Widow's Pension application and issue.

(ii) Other Documents

A variety of other documents have survived the years including:-

Birth Certificate in the name of Isaac James Elwell – *'…born on 3rd October 1879 to Joseph Benjamin Elwell and Martha Elwell (née Wassall). Joseph was a day labourer. Address – 1 Court, Upper Street, Birmingham (parish of St. George). Registered on 13th November 1879.'* [Copy obtained on 21st October 1892 for the purpose of completing the formalities for a Labour Certificate.]

Certificate of Baptism in the name of James Isaac (sic) Elwell – *'…baptised on July 21st 1889. Born on 3rd October 1879. Parents – Joseph and Martha Elwell. Living at Green Lane, Birchills, Walsall. Joseph was a labourer. Primitive Methodist, Bloxwich Parish.'*

Labour Certificate – *'3rd October 1889, James Elwell of 93, Farringt(d)on Street, Walsall, (who is) not less than 10 years of age…has received a certificate from one of Her Majesty's Inspectors of Schools, that he (James Elwell) has reached the V Standard. Reached means passed in reading, writing and arithmetic.'*

Marriage Certificate – *'Isaac James Elwell/Bertha Webster (both of Walsall). Married by Rev. John Roskell on 26 September 1908, in the presence of Sydney John Powell and Ellen (Nell) Florence Elwell. St. Patrick's RC Church, Walsall.'*

Invoice dated 7th September 1916 to Pte. J.J. Elwell, 5937, 16 Platoon, 'D' Coy, 6th South Staffs, Scotton Camp, Catterick, Yorkshire. Various items, letter cases, web belts – 21s 7d. (£1.08p) written receipt.

A card issued by Walsall War Pensions Committee in respect of a pension of five shillings per week granted to Bertha for a period of six weeks during November and December of 1918.

Original cutting from the *'Walsall…..and District, (incorporating the Walsall Advertiser).'* Saturday, May 4, 1918. Roll of Honour in Memoriam.

'In ever loving memory of my dear Husband, private I.J. Elwell, of the 7th Suffolk Regiment, who was reported killed in action on April 28th, 1917; aged 37 years.

You are not forgotten, husband dear,
Nor will you ever be;
As long as life and memory last
We shall remember thee.

Deeply mourned by his sorrowing Wife and children Lizzie and Lucy.'

(iii) Other items

A number of other items sent home from France by Jim have fortunately been preserved. These include:-

One of the more remarkable things to survive is the paper wrapping in which Jim sent home in March 1917 two crucifixes for his daughters – the pencil-written words '2 Crucifixes' are discernible on the outside.

Approximately once a month each soldier was allowed to send a letter home in a 'Green Envelope' which meant that it, '...need not be censored regimentally' and thus could contain the more personal sentiments that were difficult to include in letters that were routinely opened and read by a man's platoon officer; obviously, soldiers were put on trust to not write anything that might be of aid to an enemy. One such envelope, sent from France by Jim on 14th January 1917, has survived the years and is among the Elwell Papers.

A number of embroidered cards, very popular with the British Tommies, have survived in very good condition. Most of them carry messages such as, 'Happy Christmas' – 'To my little daughter Lucy wishing you a Merry Christmas and Happy New Year, from your soldier Daddy. Just a little card and handkerchief with best love. X,' and 'To my little daughter Lucy wishing you a very happy birthday with lots of love from your soldier daddy.'

There is also a series of seven cards sent to Bertha at Christmas 1917; one of the embroidered cards carries the words, 'To my dear wife with kind and best wishes for a Merry Xmas and a Happy New Year. From your loving Husband Jim,' and 'Just a little card and handkerchief, with best love.'

Most touching among the items is a simple card bearing the inscription, 'Birthday Greetings Across the Sea' and the handwritten message, 'Wishing dear Daddy Many Happy Returns. Much love from Betty (Jim's daughter, Lizzie).' It is superscribed, 'Found in France May 20/5/18.' This is almost certainly one of the cards that was retrieved by Private Cantillion and returned to Bertha in 1918.

There are several sets of postcards, as follows:-

Two sets of six postcards, each with a section of the Lord's Prayer. One set inscribed, 'To my little Lizzie from her soldier Daddy, with love. x.' The second inscribed, 'To my little Lucy from her soldier Daddy. x.'

One set of four cards entitled, 'The Volunteer Organist.' Signed, 'from Jim.'

One set of two cards entitled, 'I want to see the old home again.' Signed, 'from Jim.'

One set of six cards entitled, 'Remember Me' and signed, 'from Jim to Bertha.'

One set of five cards depicting a soldier and an inset of a young woman. Unsigned.

Silk-embroidered handkerchief, 'Souvenir de France.'

Two tasselled, Christmas bookmarks.

Three silk handkerchiefs, in immaculate condition, have survived. Among them are those embroidered with the words, 'Remembrance from France' and bearing the flags of five Allied nations; another carries the words, 'Souvenir de France' (pictured above) and again bearing Allied flags; another, embroidered with a bird and bright flowers bears the words, 'A kiss from the trenches'.

(iv) Photographs

Two portraits of Jim in uniform, Walsall and Richmond, Yorkshire.

Jim and Alf Walker in uniform.

Jim, Alf Walker and 13 Platoon, 6th South Staffordshire Reserve Battalion, Scotton Camp.

Jim, in uniform, with Bertha, Lizzie and Lucy.

Jim, in uniform, with Bertha, Lizzie, Lucy and Nell (Bertha's sister) – two photos.

Jim, probably on his wedding day – two photos.

Bertha, probably on her wedding day.

Jim and Bertha.

Jim and Will Simpson.

Jim and Harry Webster.

Jim with Winnie and Teresa Powell and Nell Webster.

Nell Simpson, Jim's sister.

Ted Elwell, Jim's brother, in uniform.

Ted Elwell and Nell Webster, Bertha's sister.

Sid Powell, the younger.

Will and Nell's wedding, family photo.

Joe Clifton, who married Bertha twenty years after Jim's death.

Fred and Teresa Powell in later life.

Jim Powell (senior).

MaryAnn Powell and baby Teresa.

The foundry, back of 41, Blue Lane West.]

These four photographs were kindly loaned by Alleyn Jones, great-granddaughter of Jim Powell (senior).

(v) Line-drawing

Drawing of 41 and 42, Blue Lane West

Drawn by Fred Powell, Father of Alleyn and grandson of Jim Powell (senior).

Bibliography

A. The Elwell Papers and Other Family Photographs:

Cantillion, Ethel & Henry J.– *Letters sent to Bertha, 1918.*

Elwell, Bertha, official correspondence, including:
British Red Cross. London.
Infantry Records Office, Warley.
Ministry of Pensions, Baker Street, London.
W.H. Brown, Prospective Parliamentary Candidate, Walsall Liberal Association.
Walsall War Pensions Committee.

Elwell, Bertha – *Letters sent to France and returned, April 1917.*
Elwell family photographs
Elwell, Jim – *Letters, cards and memorabilia sent from training camps and the trenches, June 1916 to April 1917.*
Jones, Alleyn – *Several Powell family photographs and extensive family information.*
Powell, Fred – *Hand-drawn sketch of the Blue Lane houses owned by Fred and Teresa Powell.*
Walker, Alf – *Letter sent to Bertha, December 1917.*

B. Books, Documents, Rolls of Honour and CD-Roms:

Battalion War Diaries *(National Archives, Kew, London).*
       - *WO95/1852 7th Battalion, the Suffolk Regiment.*
       - *WO95/2687 1/6th Battalion, the South Staffordshire Regiment.*
       - *WO95/1840 69th Field Company, Royal Engineers.*

Becke, Major E.F. – *'Order of Battle of Divisions, 1914-1918 (Parts 1, 2A, 2B, 3A, 3B)'.*
Bilton, David – *'The Home Front in the Great War'.*
Brown, Malcolm – *'Tommy Goes to War'.*
Coombs, Rose E. B. – *'Before Endeavours Fade'.*
Directory – *'Bennett's Business Directory, 1914'.*
Farndale, General Sir Martin, KCB – *'History of the Royal Regiment of Artillery - the Western Front 1914-18.'*
Gliddon, Gerald – *'Battle of the Somme – a Topographical History'.*
Gilbert, Martin – *'First World War Atlas.'*
Hardman, Robert – *'City Under the Slaughter.'* Excellent article on the Arras tunnels and caverns published in the Daily Mail on Saturday, 15th March 2008.
Holmes, Richard – *'Tommy'.*
Hurst, Sidney C. – *'The Silent Cities – A Guide to the War Cemeteries and Memorials to the Missing in France & Flanders'.*
IGN Maps – *'Institut Geographique National, Serie Verte (1 km à 1 cm)'. Sheet 04, Laon-Arras.*
James, Brigadier E.A. – *'British Regiments, 1914-1918'.*
James, Captain E.A. – *'A Record of the Battles and Engagements of the British Armies in France and Flanders, 1914-1918'.*
Jones, James P. – *'History of the South Staffordshire Regiment (1705-1923)'.*
Messenger, Charles. – *'Call to Arms – The British Army 1914-1918.'*
McCarthy, Chris – *'The Somme, 1916 – the Day-by-Day Account'.*
Ministry of Pensions – *'Location of Hospitals and Casualty Clearing Stations, British Expeditionary Force, 1914-1919'.*
National Census – *1851, 1861, 1871, 1881, 1891, 1901.*
Nicholls, Jonathan – *'Cheerful Sacrifice – Battle of Arras, 1917'.*

Official History of the Great War   – *'Military Operations, 1916, volume two (compiled by Captain Wilfrid Miles)'*.
        – *'Military Operations, 1917, volume one (compiled by Captain Cyril Falls)'*.
        – *'Military Operations, France and Belgium, 1914-1918, Maps', (CD-Rom, Naval & Military Press)*.

Rolls of Honour – *'The Staffordshire Roll of Honour' (original and print in Lichfield Cathedral)*.
        – *'St. Patrick's RC Church Roll of Honour'*.
        – *'Walsall Roll of Honour', (Walsall Town Hall)*.

Satterthwaite, Sue – *'Walsall Servicemen 1914-1918 – A Guide to Research'*.

Vale, Colonel W.L.– *'History of the South Staffordshire Regiment'*.

Walsall Corporation – *'Walsall & District Roll of the Great War'*. - *'Peace Celebrations & War Memorial, 1919'*.

Walsall Observer and South Staffordshire Chronicle – *'Walsall Observer, 1916-1921' (copies on microfilm)*.

War Office – *'Soldiers and Officers Died in the Great War', (CD-Rom version, Naval & Military Press)*.

Wayman, Ken – *'The True and Faithful Men'*.

Westlake, Ray – *'British Battalions on the Somme, 1916'*.

Winter, Denis – *'Death's Men'*.

C. Websites

Commonwealth War Graves Commission – *'Debt of Honour – Casualties.'*
        To be found at: **www.cwgc.org**

The Long, Long Trail [Chris Baker] – *'Great War Forum.'*
        To be found at: **www.1914-1918.net**

Lone poppy, Arras Memorial.

'THANK GOD I AM TRYING TO DO MY LITTLE BIT'

Printed in the United Kingdom
by Lightning Source UK Ltd.
133007UK00001B/45-46/P